Elvis Costello

An Illustrated Biography by
Mick St. Michael.

Omnibus Press
London/New York/Sydney/Cologne

Edited by Chris Charlesworth.
Cover Design & Art Direction by Mike Bell.
Co-ordinated by Lynda Hassett.
Cover Illustration by Mark Thomas.
Picture Research by Mick St. Michael.

ISBN 07119.0772.2
Order No. OP 43561

Exclusive distributors:

Book Sales Limited
78 Newman Street, London W1P 3LA, UK.

Music Sales Corporation
24 East 22nd Street, New York, NY 10010, USA.

Omnibus Press
GPO Box 3304, Sydney, NSW 2001, Australia.

To the Music Trade only:

Music Sales Limited
78 Newman Street, London W1P 3LA, UK.

Typeset by 'floppy disc transfer' by Serious Software.
Printed in Scotland by Thomson Litho, East Kilbride.

Welcome To The Working Week
Page 5

If It Ain't Stiff…
Page 20

This Year's Elvis
Page 34

Armed And Dangerous
Page 44

Soul Attractions
Page 53

An Album To Trust
Page 64

Nashville Cat
Page 74

Elvis Turns Emperor
Page 82

Bold As Brass
Page 90

Goodbye Cruel World?
Page 100

Only A Northern Folksinger
Page 113

Discography
Page 118

Elvis Costello

The Author thanks Chris, Laura, Jane Harris and John Tobler for typing, information, encouragement and sound advice – though not necessarily in that order … Plus a tip of the cap to ECIS.

Welcome To The Working Week

The Elvis Costello story begins with two men, Dave Robinson and Jake Riviera, who together founded the Stiff Records label in 1976. For both individuals, owning their own record company was the realisation of a long cherished dream. What capital they brought with them was borrowed: their real assets were street-level suss and two well thumbed telephone books full of contacts amassed over several years in the music business.

Robinson, a genial Irishman, served a tough apprenticeship as tour manager to the legendary Jimi Hendrix in the late Sixties. From this he moved to management proper with Eire Apparent, Hendrix protégés whose heyday was even briefer – and far less distinguished – than that of their mentor (their singer, Ernie Graham, was later to release a one-off single on Stiff). From there, Robinson's career diverted into the world of pop public relations via Famepushers, a forerunner of the independent publicists who marshal the media for the supergroups of the Eighties. This early venture was not a spectacular success, though, and he returned to management with Kilburn and The High Roads, featuring another future Stiff recording star in Ian Dury.

The next stop on Dave Robinson's musical mystery tour was the Hope and Anchor public house in the North London suburb of Islington. This was a major breeding ground for pub-rock, the first stage of a musical backlash against 'pomp-rock' bands like Emerson Lake and Palmer, Yes and King Crimson who, in the early Seventies, flaunted an excess of technique and technology to an audience that, although initially large, was beginning to tire of both. Though punk was to sound pomp's final death-knell, pub-rock was in many respects its forerunner. Taking most of their musical cues from the United States, quaintly-named bands like Bees Make Honey, Ducks Deluxe and Eggs Over Easy took elements of R&B and country and western to provide an energetic yet intellectually undemanding music that suited its seedy public-house venues as perfectly as light ale complements bitter. Robinson recorded a number of these groups at his 8-track Hope and Anchor studio and, when a tape from a gravel-voiced singer named Graham Parker was aired on Charlie Gillett's Radio London show, inundating the station with phone calls from record-company A&R men, Robinson deemed the time right to return to management for a third time.

Former advertising man Jake Riviera (born plain Andrew Jakeman) would undoubtedly have thrived on Robinson's Famepushers gig – the man is a born publicist and extrovert of gargantuan proportions. His intro to the music business came with the exotic-sounding Chilli Willi and The Red Hot Peppers, a band formed by much-travelled blues guitarist Martin Stone and vocalist Phil Lithman. The Willis, as they were colloquially and conveniently abbreviated, were living proof that pub-rock, like some beers, didn't travel well. Their easygoing blend of bluegrass, urban blues, country and swing could blow the roof off most hostelries, yet for all Riviera's efforts to expose them to a wider public they just could not capture the hearts of audiences outside the capital. Regular trips up and down the motorways of Britain brought little joy, yet even the post-gig stupor of a four a.m. van drive back to London couldn't extinguish Riviera's *joie de vivre*, as Andy Childs, then a *Zig Zag* fanzine writer and now a Riviera employee, remembers: "Jake was the only person exhibiting signs of life; hand on the steering wheel, eyes fixed on the road, singing and talking, trying to stay awake."

His big coup, designed to take the Willis from the pubs to a national audience in a matter of a few short weeks, was the Naughty Rhythms Tour of 1975. It was an ingenious idea – find three hopeful bands of varying styles and present them as a cut-price package. With three record companies to provide financial support, ticket prices could be pegged, too, while the acts took turns at headlining in a steal from the Stax soul revues of the Sixties. Sadly, only R&B revivalists Dr. Feelgood proved to have the visual appeal to survive transplantation onto bigger stages and venues. So it was, then, that Jake found himself in 1976 tour managing for the Feelgoods, both Kokomo and the Willis having passed on as footnotes in the pages of rock legend. But as events would later prove Jake wasn't the kind of guy to give up on a good idea just because the public couldn't recognise a bargain…

Having helped break the Feelgoods, no-one could begrudge Riviera the right to change horses and enjoy some of their success. But Jake's talents were in many ways wasted as mere tour manager. His and the Feelgoods' was a fiery relationship, and one which resulted in the factions parting company during a US tour in San Diego, California, after a bust-up over a mislaid wah-wah pedal. The split wasn't irrevocable, though; taking refuge with former Chilli Willi drummer Pete Thomas in Santa Monica, he was

subsequently reinstated. Thomas had emigrated to the West Coast

to play with former Kingston Trio mainman John Stewart and was
to resurface a short while later in an entirely different context. Back
in 1976, however, Jake was glad of his hospitality, deciding there
and then that he was going to found his own record label. Just to
show there were no hard feelings, the working capital of £400 was
supplied by none other than the Feelgoods' lead singer Lee
Brilleaux. The pattern for Riviera's project came from the
American independent labels he'd seen in every port of call,
especially San Francisco's Flat Out Records and Matthew King
Kaufman's Berserkley. If small was beautiful in the States, he
reasoned, why not in Britain?

Located behind a shopfront in Alexander Street in London's
Bayswater, Stiff Records' first office resembled a cross between
the Battle of Britain operations room and a student squat. Posters
festooned the walls, a blackboard proclaimed the day to day
movements of Stiff artists, and great piles of records threatened an
imminent vinyl avalanche. The first of these was recorded by Nick
Lowe, one of Jake's fellow travellers on the Feelgoods' first US
tour. He'd in fact been 'along for the ride' courtesy of the proceeds
of a recently signed publishing deal, but in all honesty Lowe had few
further prospects of fame and fortune on the horizon. As bassist-
vocalist and chief songwriter for Brinsley Schwarz, his career had
been in constant commercial decline ever since the band was
'launched' in New York in April 1970 by Dave Robinson's
Famepushers. Their tactic of flying over a planeload of English
journalists to see the Brinsleys open a Fillmore East show
backfired amid cries of 'hype', and the band continued with the
lowest of profiles for four more years – 'Despite It All', as one of
their album titles wryly commented – and without significant
further assistance from Robinson. So Brinsley Schwarz slipped
happily into pub-rock obscurity, mixing self-penned songs with
classic soul and country numbers, playing in jeans and workshirts,
and presenting a determined non-image to a disinterested press
and a dedicated but commercially negligible following.

Lowe had little chance to escape his old cohorts at Stiff even
if he'd wanted to, since Dave Robinson recruited two ex-Brinsleys
– eponymous guitarist Schwarz and keyboardist Bob Andrews – to
back Graham Parker in The Rumour. Robinson signed Parker to
Phonogram, and their debut album, 'Howling Wind', was to provide
Lowe with his first production credit. As he freely admitted,
though, his move from one side of the studio glass to the other was
purely with financial gain in mind. "I didn't have anything going for
me at all. I teamed up with Jake Riviera because I used to sleep on
his couch when I had nowhere to go – I stayed for about a year." So
it was that Nick Lowe became Stiff's studio Svengali.

And while the Rumour connection linked Nick to his past, he

found the time to kick off his own recording future with Stiff's first single, 'So It Goes'/'Heart Of The City', recorded in North London's Pathway Studios for the princely sum of £45. It sold 10,000 copies – not enough to put it in chart contention, perhaps, but a pretty good return on the investment. The tracks were also to appear on at least a couple of Stiff compilations, one of which boasted a Lowe/Riviera composition entitled 'I Love My Label'. Jake, ever modest, preferred to keep a low profile by crediting himself – yes, L. Profile.

Pathway Studios was to become something of a second home to Lowe who, as Stiff's house producer, used to "sit there and wait for the door to open to see who Jake had sent up there. They'd sing their song, I'd knock it into some sort of musical shape and we'd make a record. Almost anyone who had a bit of front would get a try out." With such limited resources, Stiff found the biggest problem wasn't selling the records – Jake heaved them out of his car boot and into the record shops himself – but keeping the records available for when shops re-ordered. Punk once more placed the emphasis firmly on singles as the vital currency of rock, so even if Stiff did take their name from the industry term for a record that failed to sell, the quantities they were dealing with were easy enough to dispose of.

It wasn't surprising, then, that Stiff's first singles failed to register in the national charts. But even if money was no object, the label's roster contained precious few household names. The Tyla Gang was led by ex-Ducks Deluxe singer Sean Tyla; Lew Lewis was a harmonica player from Canvey Island and a neighbour of the Feelgoods; The Pink Fairies were psychedelic refugees from the hippie era; Roogalator's R&B was recorded on the cheap at a BBC Radio 1 session.

By invoking the old pals' act Riviera and Robinson not only gave a much-needed fillip to the careers of sundry pub-rock survivors but were able to release a series of one-off singles at minimal cost and with no great commitment on either side. The only single to sell in real numbers was The Damned's 'New Rose', a Nick Lowe production later claimed to be the first punk single to be made available nationwide. It was already becoming obvious, though, that talent would have to be sought from outside the current cliquey crop if Stiff wanted to do more than just survive. Hence the appearance of a highly significant small ad in the classified columns of the weekly music press in the spring of 1977. It was time for Stiff Records and the future Elvis Costello to become acquainted.

Declan Patrick McManus. The public was fast becoming accustomed to all manner of pseudonymous performers, with names signifying their own particular soapbox. And why not? After all, John Lydon and John Mellors, who might easily have been taken for senior partners in a solicitors' practice, lost nothing by adopting Johnny Rotten and Joe Strummer as their stage names. Though Elvis' iconoclastic new forename – dreamed up by Jake (who else?) over a drink – initially proved unfortunate given the untimely demise of his better-known namesake. Costello had family connections, being his great grandmother's name. Nor was it the first time a member of the McManus clan had borrowed the monicker, as *New Musical Express* readers learned when the 'Thrills' column of that paper uncovered a version of Lennon-McCartney's 'Long And Winding Road', recorded for the Spark label in 1970 by one 'Day Costello'. A press photo was unearthed, and yes – there *was* a distinct resemblance, although it was pointed out that Elvis/Declan would have been no more than 16 at the time of recording. All was resolved when 'Day Costello' revealed his true identity a few weeks later – it was none other than Elvis' father, Ross McManus, who'd doubtless been flattered by the media attention.

From him, too, came the eagerly awaited first details of Declan's upbringing, hitherto jealously guarded by the man himself. From these, and from his subsequent more relaxed exchanges with the press, it was possible to sketch an outline of his early life. Born in St Mary's Hospital, Paddington, London, on 25 August 1954, the only child of Ronald (Ross) and Lillian McManus, he was nominally brought up a Catholic. The last two salient facts alone would provide many a rock journalist with a hotly-sought 'key' to Costello's complexes, while the fact that his parents separated when he was very young would probably be greeted equally eagerly by those amateur psychologists.

The oft-used cliché that music ran in the family could hardly have been more true for the youngster. His father joined Joe Loss' orchestra in 1955 as featured vocalist and was to stay 14 years, while his mother ran the record department at Selfridge's department store on Oxford Street in London's West End. Though both parents were musically inclined, they were careful not to push the youngster too hard, with the result that he never learned to read music, a fact he later publicly regretted. What was perhaps better than over-encouragement was the fact that Declan was brought up in a house full of music.

Initially the predominant sound was jazz, as Ross worked with such luminaries as Ronnie Scott, Tubby Hayes and Phil Seaman. Yet in the early Sixties the pop world was very much part of the middle-class showbiz tradition – up-and-coming beat groups like The Mojos, Merseybeats, Hollies and even The Beatles and Rolling Stones appeared on the Joe Loss Show on Friday lunchtimes, rubbing shoulders with Declan and his dad in the dressing room. While Mrs. McManus' tastes remained rooted in the jazz and ballads of Sinatra and Fitzgerald, her husband was required to render the pop hits of the day with orchestral backing, and he brought home acetate (pre-release) copies to learn the latest sounds. The two strands of jazz and beat were later to surface in Costello's music, and many of the cover versions he still plays date from this time.

Educated in Catholic schools until the age of 11, Declan commenced his secondary education in the West London suburb of Hounslow under the flight path of Heathrow Airport. Never a high flyer in the scholastic sense, he nevertheless obtained one GCE A level – not unsuprisingly, in view of later events, in English. By that time he'd moved back to Liverpool with his mother, his parents having separated. Ross also split from Joe Loss in 1969; doubling on trumpet and piano, he continues to this day to play the Northern club circuit where he's quite a 'draw', periodically bumping into his son at Watford Gap services on the way home.

While records from the early Seventies might have lacked the cultural clout of the mid Sixties, they still provided a varied soundtrack for the life of a teenager such as McManus, a fact reflected in the many echoes that have since surfaced in his later work. Party dance music was provided by the 'Motown Chartbusters' singles compilations and their reggae counterpart, the 'Tighten Up' series. Rather than hitch himself to the glam-rock bandwagon of groups like T. Rex, Gary Glitter and The Sweet, the youngster opted for the wave of introspective singer songwriters – Randy Newman, James Taylor – which filled the gap in American music between the progressive Sixties and the soft-rock Seventies.

A self-confessed loner as a schoolkid, any musical ambitions Declan fostered were, at this stage, confined solely to himself – and for a young man with an acoustic guitar and a clutch of self-penned songs the folk clubs seemed as good a place to start as any. The tradition of floor singers, members of the audience who'd get up to do a 'turn' during the interval before the main attraction, gave many nervous performers the chance to cut their teeth before an audience – and though he later recalled that his first appearance in a London club in 1969 sent celebrated folk songwriter Ewan MacColl to sleep, he persevered.

Fairport Convention was one of the more influential groups of the day, and they provided young McManus with a certain amount of inspiration. The longest-lived of all electric folk bands, they'd been one of the first in Britain to discover Dylan and make the electric guitar all but acceptable in folk circles, and they even had a hit single ('Si Tu Dois Partir' – Dylan's 'If You Gotta Go', strangely translated into French). Their lead guitarist, Richard Thompson, left in 1971 to follow a solo career, teaming up shortly afterwards with Linda Peters, whom he married. Some of the songs he wrote and recorded in the next few years were later to find their way into the Elvis Costello/Imposter repertoire.

Back in the early Seventies, though, Declan McManus was still very much open to influences of all kinds. And it wasn't just for musical reasons that he was attracted to The Band – and particularly bassist/vocalist Rick Danko, whose unique vocal style he was keen to emulate. "They didn't look pretty," he later said. "It appealed to me that they looked really ugly." The Band acquired their name through their role as backing musicians for Bob Dylan, another McManus favourite. Thoughts of recruiting a band of his own came to little until Declan left school, moved to London and became a founding member of Flip City.

Most of what has been written about Flip City has been speculative and/or misleading due to their comparative anonymity at the time. Indeed, had their frontman not found fame and fortune later they would probably have remained in the total obscurity enjoyed by most of their semi-pro pub-rock contemporaries. The extensive mid-Seventies circuit of clubs, pubs and colleges in London provided limitless opportunities for young musicians. The monetary rewards on offer might not have constituted boundless riches – £20 a night was the going rate for two 45-minute sets – but for a band whose members had 'day jobs' it was a welcome contribution towards the expenses that inevitably cropped up.

Few star names came out of pub-rock – Ian Dury, Nick Lowe and Dr. Feelgood were honourable exceptions – but the style was one of the simplest and most enjoyable you could find. Despite massive critical indifference, it was certainly true that a chance visit to your 'local' could yield the soundtrack for an entertaining evening – no more, perhaps, but rarely less.

Flip City's five-piece line-up consisted of Michael 'Mich' Kent (bass), Dickie Faulkner (congas and percussion), Malcolm Dennis (drums), Steve Hazelhurst (lead guitar) and Declan McManus (rhythm guitar and vocals). They came together as a result of a chance meeting between Mich and Dec, as he preferred to be known, at a Brinsley Schwarz gig at St. Pancras Town Hall in the summer of 1973. Having decided to put a band together, the two teamed up with Malcolm Dennis, an old school friend of Mich's and played a number of tentative dates at South London venues (including Wimbledon's Southlands College) as the unfortunately-named Mothertruckers before changing their handle to The Bizario Brothers and, finally, Flip City.

The new name came courtesy of McManus' girlfriend Mary Burgoyne, whom he'd met at school and who, after a spell at teacher training college in Liverpool, had dropped out and moved south. One of her favourite albums was Joni Mitchell's 'Court and Spark', and it was Mitchell's reading of Annie Ross's 'Twisted' – with assistance from those stoned satirists Cheech and Chong – that yielded the name. "That chick is twisted. Crazy…flip city," muttered Cheech – or was it Chong? – and the band was promptly re-christened. Not everyone was convinced about the name at first, but a little bit of publicity helped decide things. John Collis, music critic for London listings magazine *Time Out,* ran a publicity picture of them (taken by a friend) that had been sent more in hope than expectation, while journalist/record company boss/disc jockey Charlie Gillett was in the habit of publicising bands' dates on his Radio London programme 'Honky Tonk'. So when 'Flip City' received their mention on the air the name just *had* to stick.

The band couldn't stay a three-piece for long – Declan was a reasonable rhythm guitarist, but vocals and lead guitar was quite a load for his diminutive frame to carry. A friend, Dickie Faulkner, was drafted in primarily to supply backing vocals and he brought his congas (an unusual instrument for pub-rock bands) with him. The next step was to find a lead guitarist. The final choice, Steve Hazlehurst, had already been auditioned and rejected before he was finally invited to join the band after their first choice turned out to be something of a 'dopehead'. Unlike their Sixties predecessors, pub-rockers tended to live up to their name by deriving energy and inspiration primarily from the fruit of the hop.

Steve was the only member of the band to get a solo spot in the set, all other lead vocal duties falling to Declan. Unusually for such a large group McManus was the only writer, the set being made up of a mixture of self-penned songs and cover versions he'd selected. Yet as Laura Marcus, friend of the band points out, there was no resentment. "It wasn't his band, but he was always the dominating factor, the driving force. He also did the least amount of humping gear, due to his 'bad back' – but I guess that's what they call artistic temperament. He was totally, utterly and unquestioningly dedicated. He had no doubt that he was going to make it…it was just a question of time. It was a dream to the others, but for him it was a definite ambition."

Rock stars of the Sixties made fashionable the communing with nature first practised by Steve Winwood and Traffic, 'getting it together in the country' away from the distractions of city dwelling. When three members of Flip City (Dec, Mich and Malcolm) plus sound mixer Mike Whelan decided to rent a house in Roehampton Vale late in 1973 geographical convenience was perhaps the factor uppermost in their minds. Yet if the hippie term 'commune' had been shortened from community, Number 3 Stag Lane was certainly that – for boys in their late teens and early twenties who shared the same interests and enjoyed each other's company.

All the band members had day jobs, a necessary evil to pay the £32 per month rent, keep body and soul together and finance their musical activities. Drummer Malcolm had the 'best' job, working with musical instruments at the Fender soundhouse in central London, while Steve was a van driver, Mich a toolmaker and Dickie a maintenance man. Declan was working with computers for the Elizabeth Arden cosmetics firm – 'the vanity factory' that was to surface on his first album. Whatever his feelings about the job in retrospect, it gave him ample opportunity for songwriting; he'd often come home from shifts with screeds of lyrics written on computer paper. Needless to say, shift work was never allowed to interfere with rehearsals or gigs. "He had a lot of time off sick," a friend remembers. It wasn't all in the mind, either. Working under artificial light and constantly looking at figures or VDU screens tended to cause him headaches, and Declan adopted a pair of peardrop-shaped tinted spectacles for occasional use; this was the first time anyone had seen him wearing glasses. There is no evidence to suggest that Declan – or Elvis – ever *had* to wear glasses for optical reasons.

Declan's frustration with having to work for a living was to fuel his creative muse on more than one occasion. If 'Welcome To The Working Week' on his first album is the best-known of these songs, then its forerunner was 'Sweet Revival', a standout of the Flip City originals. 'I get the weekend, they get the rest,' ran the lyric. But at least living with his fellow musicians made arrangements and rehearsals relatively easy. And since the band had originally got together under the eclectic umbrella of Brinsley Schwarz, it was hardly surprising that musical crazes tended to hit the house *en masse* – someone would bring a record which would be played to death and sooner or later have its own influence on the band's music.

The musical alumni of 1974 were almost exclusively American. Little Feat (whose 'Cold, Cold, Cold' was occasionally essayed as a cover) and The Grateful Dead were staples, while Flip City and friends discovered Bruce Springsteen long before his music – or the attendant barrage of hype – was heard in most British living-rooms. Indeed, the fact that Springsteen's career was nearly ruined by an insensitive marketing campaign (built around the slogan 'At last the world is ready for Bruce Springsteen') helped shape Dec's future negative attitude towards publicity.

Released in 1973, Springsteen's first album, 'Greetings From Asbury Park NJ', had a profound effect on Flip City's young singer. Like McManus, Bruce had a tendency to pack rather too many words into his songs, yet seemed to get away with it. And the advent of his more fully realised second album, 'The Wild, The

Innocent and The E Street Shuffle', later in the year sparked an immediate response. 'Radio Soul', written in early 1974, bore the unmistakable Springsteen stamp, with a clipped rhythm-guitar intro and celebratory release in the lyrics. A visitor to the house hearing the band's new material about this time commented, "It's like 'Greetings From Stag Lane' here."

As Declan became more self-conscious of his own writing, he rearranged the song to divest it of its more obvious influences. Yet even at one of the band's last gigs Flip City could still play it "the old way" for one of their followers. This wasn't the last that was to be heard of the song either – not by a long chalk. Nearly five years on, when the world had tuned into its composer, 'Radio Soul' had become 'Radio Radio' and Declan McManus had become Elvis Costello. But that was all in the future.

Despite diligent research, rock historians have yet to discover any live reviews of Flip City's gigs – and no wonder, for the breadth of their self-penned and 'borrowed' material must have made them the proverbial critic's nightmare. Of the cover versions some were rock standards with a country flavour – Dylan's 'Knockin' On Heaven's Door' and Little Feat's 'Willin'', while others like 'Third-Rate Romance' (from Jesse Winchester's repertoire) were just plain obscure. Yet what else could you expect from a bunch of scruffy-looking American music fanatics who even intended one of their publicity stills as a take-off of a Barefoot Jerry album cover? Flip City, like so many bands of their time, were primarily *enthusiasts*, and it came over in their music. Stage presence, stage clothes and other such niceties were for the birds.

Van Morrison, another (adopted) American with a way with words, was also a band favourite at the time. Their arrangement of Sam Cooke's 'Bring It On Home To Me' was not dissimilar, in fact, to Morrison's own played live in London in 1973 and released on the live LP 'It's Too Late To Stop Now', and was one of McManus' most impassioned performances. 'Bring It On Home' was often placed back to back with another Cooke number, 'Another Saturday Night', which didn't quite offer the same vocal scope. Declan himself chose the cover versions in what a friend called "a democratic dictatorship" – the others were quite happy to abide by his musical judgement. "It wasn't so much he imposed the ideas, he was the one who *had* the ideas," remembers Laura Marcus. "The others went along with them."

The band's gigs had up to now been fairly low-key; like many groups before and since they'd be prepared to play for little financial reward and only the dream of stardom for motivation. Pub-rock even made the charts when Ace scored with 'How Long' in late 1974, so it wasn't beyond the realms of possibility that Flip City might someday reach a wider audience. But for now it was enough to have a good time, with well-known covers like Hank Williams' country classic 'You Win Again' and Dylan's 'It Takes A Train To Laugh' giving the crowds every incentive to dance. The latter was to become Steve Hazelhurst's vocal number, with Declan taking over lead guitar chores – not too convincingly, it must be said.

Flip City's appearance as advertised at their many and various venues depended solely on the sound mechanical order of a Ford van purchased second hand for the princely sum of £20 – a night's work. Friends, too, played a big part in keeping the show on the road; Ken Smith acted as manager, but the sound mixing, gear humping and – most important of all – moral support came from others.

The band's policy of playing anywhere and everywhere took them to some unusual locations. Perhaps the furthest afield they ventured was an American college near Maidenhead, Berkshire, while a Greek folk club called The Howff in St. John's Wood welcomed them back more than once. A booking at a bikers' pub, The Gun in southeast London, looked like it could lead to trouble, as Laura Marcus remembers. "Dec just sat down and said 'Let's sort out the set', but I was sure it was going to be a terrible evening – I was actually scared. But Dec just started chatting to some guy who said he could play harmonica and invited him to come up and have a blow. The result was the audience all loved him. That was an example of his common touch."

The five members of Flip City briefly became six when a pianist named Nick was recruited via a music-press small ad that mentioned the Grateful Dead, Little Feat and The Band as cross-references to their music. His arrival (and subsequent departure) was far from the only change going on: Malcolm Dennis was replaced on drums in 1975 by Ian Powell. The end was in sight, too, for Stag Lane. March 1975 saw the base of operations move to East Molesey, with percussionist Dickie now a fully paid-up resident.

By this time Declan had moved out, having married Mary in November of the previous year. Since moving south, she'd been working as a ground hostess at nearby Heathrow Airport. They were living in a flat in Twickenham, below his father Ross and second wife Sarah, when their son Matthew was born in January 1975. The gigs continued, though, seldom reaching beyond London and the home counties but with a number of venues calling them back for return gigs or residencies. On occasions when they were booked by smaller venues unused to an electric band or, a folk-oriented club like the Rising Sun on London's Tottenham Court Road, Declan would go on first and play a short acoustic set. Yet pub audiences were seldom the most attentive and, while the rest of the band were apt to ignore this and fumble about between numbers, Declan often gave as good as he got. "He'd be so rude;

he'd just *glare* at them," remembers one onlooker.

When the band was required to play two sets in one evening, it was the second set that tended to contain the most impressive numbers. It usually opened with a McManus original, 'Pay It Back', which he was later to consider worthy of a place on his first album in substantially similar form. An early reggae influence was discernible in the radically reworked 'One More Heartache', written by Smokey Robinson and a hit for Motown's Marvin Gaye now transformed into a kind of bluebeat shuffle. 'Flatfoot Hotel', another composition by Declan, contained some mysterious lyrics: 'You start up as a good guy and end up as a thief,' declared its composer who, when asked by the other band members what the song was about would only say "The point of this song is that there *is* no point." It was suggested, though, that the hotel of the title was the Royal Charter in Kingston, commonly known as 'The Fishes' and a mecca for South London hippies at the time.

Despite the fact that he was no longer a resident and wasn't around quite as often, there was no indication that Declan was anything less than 'one of the lads'. Although he wasn't a heavy drinker and was never known to take drugs, he knew how to enjoy himself – and with four young men in their early twenties living together there were always plenty of practical jokes to be played of the toothpaste-on-doorhandle variety. Yet under the surface he was a man of many parts, as Laura Marcus remembers. "He could play the devil's advocate, deliberately take the opposing view for the hell of it," she recalls. All-night debates (later recalled in the second verse of 'Radio Radio') were not uncommon, with Declan's left-of-centre political views well to the fore. Yet though he opposed abortion, he declared himself pro-feminist and could in no way be described as a male chauvinist. Add to this a passion for football and Liverpool FC in particular and you have an interesting – if paradoxical – character indeed.

In addition to gigs in their own right in the pubs, Flip City was also invited to support more established acts as their modest reputation grew. The most celebrated of these, in retrospect, was at the Marquee Club in London's Soho, where they warmed up for pub-rockers-made-good Dr. Feelgood in 1975. Future Costello confidant Nick Kent from *New Musical Express* was so keen to talk to the headliners' Wilko Johnson that he completely ignored the support act and their singer. He would receive his come-uppance in print later.

It was at another Ewell Technical College (now the North East Surrey College of Technology) supporting set that Flip City played their last gig in December 1975. No one reason could be found for the split; as much as anything, perhaps, the fun seemed to have gone out of it. The final gig with The Climax Blues Band was an acrimonious affair. "Everyone was rowing and fighting," remembered a bystander. Funnily enough, the previous month had seen the band play a relatively successful four-Sunday residency at the Red Cow, Hammersmith, the London pub venue that launched acts as successful and diverse as The Jam and AC/DC. But time had run out for Flip City.

The band played the last of their Red Cow residency dates on Sunday 30 November 1975. It had been a nostalgic occasion with the band celebrating by inviting former drummer Malcolm Dennis up to play on their first set closer, The Grateful Dead's 'Gone Dead Train'. Current sticksman Ian Powell picked up a spare guitar as he joined Dec and Steve in what they called their "Blue Oyster Cult impression with five guitars – or at least four." Yet this jokey, pub-rock irreverence now sat uneasily with the intensity of some of Declan's self-penned numbers – and nowhere was his potential more in evidence than on 'Imagination', an impassioned ballad that was in many ways a direct ancestor of 'Alison'. "Imagination is a powerful deceiver/when you try to believe her just a little too much," ran the lyrics. The tortured climax to the song was capable of reducing the clamour of *any* public house to a muted whisper, as McManus agonised. "Turn out the light so you can tell me the truth," he howled over and over – and for one moment the Red Cow stood hushed and attentive. It was a sign of things to come.

The remaining members of the band kept the house at East Molesey going until mid 1976, but musical activity was sporadic even though everyone kept in touch. Steve Hazelhurst recorded his own demo tape, and was depressed at the pile of rejection slips he amassed when sending it to record companies. "I frame all mine," laughed an unperturbed Declan, who accepted the process as an inevitable part of the rocky road towards stardom. As far as his own steps along that narrow and tortuous byway were concerned, he intended to travel light with only his acoustic guitar for company. Thus D.P. Costello, folk singer, was born.

The change of name was accompanied by a complete change of repertoire. As far as the monicker went, he later claimed he'd borrowed it from his great- grandmother because it "ran easier on the phone…there were too many hard consonants in the name McManus". And as for the songs it was definitely a case of ringing out the old with 1975 and ringing in the new – the output on Elizabeth Arden's computer paper was a long way from drying up. One cover version he retained from the old days was 'Another Saturday Night', but there were many new songs. One, 'Wave A White Flag', was particularly interesting in providing background to the charges of misogyny levelled at McManus/Costello during his first two albums. In black comic fashion, it cast the narrator as a wife-beater, the lyric snarling: "I'd love to grab you by the neck and see which way it turns." By the time of 'White Knuckles' on the 'Trust' album five years later, the public had got used to Costello's lyrical twists (no pun intended); for a folk singer in 1976 it was heavy stuff indeed.

When Flip City recorded a demo tape the previous year, the object of the exercise had been to help them secure live engagements – hence the inclusion of such crowd-pleasing covers as Chris Kenners' 'I'm Packing Up' and Dylan's 'Knocking On Heaven's Door' among the McManus originals. Now he no longer had to rely on a band, McManus/Costello tried a different tack by bearding record-company A&R men in their dens. "I used to make embarrassing scenes," he admitted. "I used to get a guitar and say, 'What do you think of this song?' I actually did force a few people to be bored for 20 minutes." The tactic wasn't exactly a roaring success, though. "It was particularly embarrassing when you're in the middle of a song and you really think you're convincing the guy and suddenly the phone goes off and he says 'Yes, yes, darling, we'll have supper at eight…'"

Even Stiff's Nick Lowe would have found the prospect unnerving. "It's the most intimidating and awe-inspiring thing to happen, because he's extremely loud, as if he's singing through a great PA to thousands of people and he's only three feet away from you. You don't know how to react." He wasn't the only one…

Yet as 1976 progressed, D.P. Costello must have had the feeling that perhaps he hadn't. Playing solo gigs around London – the Half Moon in Putney, the Swan in Kingston – he could see Graham Parker, perhaps the most notable pre-new-wave singer to come out of UK rock, achieving success with a similar brand of impassioned rock. And if both singers were later to be extravagantly compared to Dylan, then Costello was playing the undiscovered folksinger in Greenwich Village to Parker's 'Blonde On Blonde' period electric performer. Like Parker, Costello appeared on Charlie Gillett's 'Honky Tonk' radio show. But while Parker's studio demo brought immediate record-company interest, Costello's offering, home-taped on a domestic recorder, was only to acquire a retrospective value when Gillett later offered it as a prize in a competition.

The tape contained six songs, three of which were later to turn up in different forms. 'Blame It On Cain' and 'Mystery Dance' (with an extra verse) both showed on his first album, while 'Jump Up', 'Poison Moon' and the previously mentioned 'Wave A White Flag' didn't. The most interesting of the half-dozen offerings, though, was 'Cheap Reward', a song that combined some of the lyrics of 'Lip Service' with a country tune that was later to become 'Stranger In The House'. Bootlegs of the tape, logically entitled

'The Honky Tonk Demos', have become much sought-after in recent years, but back in 1976 its broadcast on 15 August excited little attention.

Undaunted, the newly-christened D.P. Costello continued on his solo way where he'd left off in Liverpool some years before, but now playing pubs, clubs and colleges south of Watford and as often as not in the middle of nowhere. And even his faithful followers from Flip City days were beginning to have their doubts. "We used to drive him to gigs," says Laura Marcus, "'cos he'd never learned to drive. It was real nickel and dime stuff. I used to feel for him. It's like seeing someone on the stage in a show that's not doing very well: they didn't understand or appreciate him." And even at that stage the shades of Graham Parker were looming even larger. "People would say 'Oh this guy's ripping off Graham Parker' and we'd say 'No, – he's really good. Just listen'."

But few did – then.

If It Ain't Stiff...

It was time for the newly-christened Elvis Costello's very first venture onto vinyl. And if that has to rank as potentially the most thrilling event of a musician's life, there can be little more disheartening than to find the title of your debut release misrepresented in its first review. 'Half Past Zero', as *New Musical Express* reviewer Charles Shaar Murray (or more likely his sub editor) contrived to put it, was "a great record (which) doesn't have a snowball's chance in hell" of being a hit. The review does deserve some kind of recognition, though, for compressing the record's 'influences' – Graham Parker, Bruce Springsteen, Phil Lynott and Billy Swan – into two column inches: was this a record? "I was just releasing singles and I wasn't a professional musician," Elvis later confessed. "I remember it being very demoralising, feeling that my only contact with the world was those singles, and those people who I didn't know or I'd never met had the make or break of it...that was very depressing."

By May, when 'Alison' came out, they were at least getting his song titles right. If Costello's career had ended right there and then, he would have left the pop music world that much richer for his presence. The song was a classic, an understated ballad sung for someone who used to be a lover and is now something less than a friend. Once a participant in the action, the singer is now left on the sidelines as the fortunes of his former love continue to slide downhill. The song's intensely personal nature hardly helped its chart chances at a time when communal emotions seemed far more fashionable; besides, a song as downbeat as *this* by an unknown artist was unlikely to walk onto the playlist of bright, bouncy national radio. Yet the fact that a line from its chorus supplied the title of Elvis' first album underlined how important this song was to its author, and it remains one of his greatest compositions eight years or more later.

When Declan McManus (also known as D. P. Costello) delivered his tape to Stiff headquarters, the first reaction was disin-

terest. But 'Mystery Dance', the most uptempo number of the set
and something of a Fifties pastiche, caught the ear of Jake Riviera
who thought that Dave Edmunds, whose career he was guiding at
that time, might fancy recording it. Then Nick Lowe arrived to give
a second opinion. "I got up to the office and Jake was saying, 'This
tape is fantastic.' He was going to sign him as a writer. We listened
to the tape a bit more and he decided to sign him as an actual artist."

So how come Stiff netted Costello when all the other labels
passed? The answer lay in the fact that the kind of artists Jake and
Dave Robinson had in mind to record were song-oriented. "They
were singing what you might term a basic rock 'n' roll, or rhythm
and blues or country-style music," explained Dave. "Most of them
were involved in a kind of fairly basic song/band structure where
there were lots and lots of songs, and that's what I've always been
interested in." So if Jake Riviera took time to get used to the idea of
Elvis Costello the performer, D.P. Costello the songwriter was
one fish he wasn't going to throw back into the pool.

Stiff had been founded fairly and squarely on gimmicks –
picture sleeves, slogans (including the infamous 'If It Ain't Stiff It
Ain't Worth A Fuck'), eye-catching adverts, silly messages on the
labels (Nick Lowe produced Costello's first album for 'Keepitasa-
hobby Productions') and scratched between the records' runoff
grooves. In keeping with that image, there was apparently a plan to
record Costello on one side of an album with Wreckless Eric (real
name Eric Goulden), Hull's answer to the diminutive Declan, playing Norman Wisdom to Costello's Woody Allen on the other.
Thankfully, this was soon dropped and Elvis found himself spending
all his free time between shifts at Elizabeth Arden recording his
very own debut album at Pathway.

Apart from the release of 'Alison', May was the merry
month when a single performance seemed to catch the imagination
not only of Jake Riviera but the music business in general. Elvis was
booked on the 27th to support The Rumour at London's Nashville
Rooms – an ironic juxtaposition, given the number of occasions that
the name of Graham Parker had already been invoked in his short
career. With The Rumour promoting their 'solo' album, 'Max', that
night, Costello had the field to himself and proceeded to make the
most of it. Standing alone with his antiquated sunburst Fender
Jazzmaster he left the place, as one onlooker put it, "in breathless
pandemonium". A new-found confidence, a new name and the
backing of 'The world's most flexible record label' seemed to be
paying dividends – and the real payoff was waiting in the wings.

Released two months later in July, 'My Aim Is True' leapt
from the racks, both literally and metaphorically, for it sold 11,000
copies in its first three days. Its most eye-catching attribute was
the Barney Bubbles-designed cover – a full-length portrait of a

bespectacled, pigeon-toed Costello clutching his guitar, looking several million miles away from the public's idea of a rock star and considerably nearer to a place in a hospital ward. Forget the title – this fellow looked like he'd find it hard to aim a paper aeroplane, let alone a punch in love *or* anger.

The knockout blow, though, came with the music: 13 tracks totalling little more than half an hour's entertainment, yet no less satisfying for that. The problem of backing musicians was neatly solved when Jake Riviera selected Clover, an American band he co-managed with Dave Robinson. Robinson, as Clover lead singer Huey Lewis remembers, spotted them in their native California before offering to bring them to England. "Jake and Dave went partners on Clover, and then started Stiff three or four weeks later. Then Elvis Costello walked in off the streets." Picking out the American influences in Costello's demos, Riviera made a snap decision: "Clover are American – we'll have them back you up."

Clover were no strangers to Costello: three years earlier he had bought their album 'Forty-Niner', and 'Mister Moon' from it was a regular Flip City cover. For their part Clover had already worked with Nick Lowe demoing material for an album ('Unavailable', later recorded with Robert 'Mutt' Lange), and were both experienced and keen to supplement their income. The rhythm section of Mickey Shine (drums) and John Ciambotti (bass) played throughout, while guitarist John McFee shared six-string duties with Costello. As for Huey Lewis, he had other ideas: "I took a vacation. I could have sung a bit or played a bit of harmonica, but we'd been on the road since 1970…" Since he ended 1984 with a US Number 1 album and a clutch of hit singles under his belt as lead singer with The News, missing out on the session doesn't seem to have harmed his career.

Musically, any Flip City fan who got past the punky packaging would have found a far more familiar set of sounds than they might at first have feared. John McFee's country-rock guitar licks weren't a million miles away from Steve Hazelhurst, while the rhythm section rarely rose above pub-rock standards in inspiration. By the end of the year, the hooks would be coming from the keyboards, not lead guitar, with the double punch of an experienced UK rhythm team turning middleweight songs into championship contenders.

As Costello bounded out of his corner with 'Welcome To The Working Week' he knew he was dealing the death-blow to his semi-professional status: soon the 'vanity factory' he sneeringly refers to in 'I'm Not Angry' would be a thing of the past. Elvis *was* angry, confused and bitter, the emotions excluding any hint of the self-pity that James Taylor and his like had once marketed so successfully. Flip City's 'Pay It Back' slotted perfectly into the prevailing mood: revenge and guilt, as Costello memorably quoted, were the only emotions he was interested in. He certainly couldn't be accused of not making his point – not once but several times. Key phrases kept recurring: 'Blame It On Cain' and 'Mystery Dance', two tracks from 'The Honky Tonk Demos', both stressed that their author was 'not satisfied', while dancing as a metaphor for sex cropped up a second time in the self-explanatory 'No Dancing'. Certainly, the knock-kneed geek holding the guitar on the cover looked as if he'd have trouble with either activity.

Only on 'Red Shoes' was Elvis content to forget his obsessions and complexes while John McFee laid down a catchy 'My Back Pages'-style guitar pattern and Costello sang like a Byrd: this *had* to be a single. Together with 'Working Week', 'Red Shoes' was probably the Elvis track most imitated by others in later months. But Costello could imitate, too, when it suited him: 'Mystery Dance' expressed frustration and fury in a Fifties setting, with Jerry Lee Lewis piano, reverbed vocals and plenty of stops and starts. In concert it was to be transformed into more of a 'Peggy Sue' by Pete Thomas' nonstop drumming, but for now it underlined the sad plight of an overgrown adolescent who's thumbed through every dirty magazine in the shop yet is left wondering, 'What's the use in looking when you don't know what it means?'

With Steve Nieve still as yet undiscovered, keyboards didn't yet play a crucial role in Costello's music; Huey Lewis, who should know, insists that Clover's Sean Hopper played on the sessions, but Elvis has credited Stan Show of The Hitmen with organ. Whatever the truth it was left to John McFee to improvise all the hooks – and this he did masterfully, especially the spooky slide guitar with which he conjured up a requisite hint of uneasiness on 'Waiting For The End Of The World'. Yet the album's lack of ornamentation – even the backing vocals, with Nick Lowe joining in the choruses, seemed to be no more than sparing – just served to emphasise the fact that whether expressing his feelings in the first person ('Miracle Man') or observing other people's problems ('No Dancing'), Costello was clearly already a songwriter of some promise. But to paraphrase the catchy chorus of 'Sneaky Feelings', he still had a long way to go…

No sooner was the album completed than it was time to find Elvis a band. With Clover – a pre-Stiff acquisition – already signed to Phonogram, there was never any question of putting Huey Lewis out of work. And besides, a two-month delay while Stiff tied up a distribution deal with Island, a larger independent, was to give Jake all the breathing space he needed to build his protégé a new-wave supergroup. Dave Robinson had paired Graham Parker with The Rumour – what would Jake come up with?

Former Chilli Willi drummer Pete Thomas flew home from his West Coast exile ostensibly to join ex-Feelgood guitarist Wilko Johnson's new band with his old colleague Paul 'Bassman' Riley. That particular ménage à trois lasted just a week before he defected to the Costello camp, leaving poor Wilko wondering what had hit him (apart from the cost of an air ticket).

The bass vacancy proved harder to fill, so Elvis borrowed The Rumour's Andrew Bodnar to help out at auditions. One of the musicians to answer the ad for a 'pop combo' in *Melody Maker* was Bruce Thomas (no relation to Pete), who cited Graham Parker and Steely Dan as his musical influences. "Forget it," came the answer – but Bruce wasn't going to take *that* lying down. Having learned the identity of the mystery act, he got hold of a pre-release copy of 'My Aim Is True' and committed John Ciambotti's bass parts to memory before returning to the fray. This time he passed muster.

There were fewer problems selecting a keyboard player – though Steve Nason's credentials for playing pop music were slim to say the least. Having studied composition at the Royal College of Music, he cheerfully admitted, "The only rock albums I ever owned were by T. Rex and Alice Cooper. The only concert I ever saw was Alice Cooper. That was great, that was." And as for 'My Aim Is True', well, Steve just "couldn't stand it…" That the feeling from the album's creator was far from mutual can be taken as read.

Nason's decision to adopt Steve Naive – later modified (as spelled throughout this book) to Nieve – as his stage name, was, in pop music terms, more than a little apt. But the contrast between the young keyboard player and the two Thomases was to prove one of the great strengths of this band in years to come.

Born in Sheffield in 1954, Pete Thomas – who is unusually tall for a drummer – misspent his youth in such schoolboy groups as the evocatively-named Surfriders (with whom he made his first live appearance, age 9, in the local village hall) and the less felicitously christened Grobs. A two-year stint with Chilli Willi, his first professional job, versed him in the art of American music to such an extent that he walked straight into John Stewart's band a seasoned pro with all styles at his fingertips.

In terms of experience, Bruce Thomas was even more of a veteran. His first appearance on record occurred as far back as 1969 with ex-Them keyboard player Pete Bardens before cutting his teeth with Bodast (with Steve Howe on guitar) and Cambridge-based soft-rockers Quiver who recorded two albums for Warner Brothers in the early Seventies. Their link with songwriting siblings The Sutherland Brothers (authors of Rod Stewart's 'Sailing') brought rather more commercial success for both parties, but met with less approval from Bruce who departed the band after their 1973 release 'Dream Kid', a sharp exchange of views in the music press ending that particular chapter of his career.

He also became a respected session player, "scratching a living in the armpit of popular music" as he later called it. His early to mid Seventies credits include albums by a veritable who's who of folk-rock performers: Marc Ellington, Jonathan Kelly, Ian Matthews, Bridget St. John and Al Stewart. His most recent attempt to play in a full-time band prior to joining Costello's crew was as one-quarter of Moonrider, a combo fronted by 'Teenage Opera' singer Keith West who was accompanied by two other veterans in ex-Animals/Family guitarist John Weider and drummer Chico Greenwood. Their one self-named album, released in 1975, was as tasteful as most of Bruce's early work without standing any chance whatsoever of selling in appreciable quantities.

Bruce's first serious band since jumping on stage to play harmonica with a schoolboy outfit named The Tremors was The Roadrunners, a group featuring Paul Rodgers (later of Free) in his native Northeast; this was spring 1967. That list of session credits attests to his ability, but anyone who thinks his distinctive playing style is a recent development should listen to Quiver's self-named debut album released in 1971. Although Bruce's upfront style, tossing in lightning-fast runs to enliven even the most unremarkable song, is the saving grace of what was a pleasant but less than gripping album of soft rock, his recording debut as a songwriter with the imaginatively titled 'On The Road' – sample lyric 'I'm so glad to be back on the road again' – wasn't so hot. While excavating skeletons from Bruce Thomas' musical closet, mention must be made of 'Queens Park Rangers', the football-chant theme song he wrote for the club of the same name in his adopted Shepherd's Bush and released in 1977. At least Elvis could rest easy in the knowledge that his pre-eminence as a lyricist remained unchallenged.

You might have thought an inexperienced youth like Steve Nieve would be overawed in such company – far from it. And for Costello, his young keyboardist's voyage of discovery through pop music's many influences was nothing less than a refreshing inspiration. "One week he discovers Booker T and the MGs, the next week he'll say 'Have you ever heard this album?' and it's 'Hard Day's Night'. He's that bit younger than the rest of the old cronies in the band…"

You could have said it was an attraction of opposites, for the new band was immediately christened The Attractions. And the aptness of that name was soon to be put to the test. "At last – Elvis To Tour" trumpeted *Melody Maker*: but a closer look at that publication, dated 23 July 1977, might well enlighten anyone who had visions of Elvis and his new-found soulmates sharing column inches with persons of a punk persuasion. No, the chart rundown in the week 'My Aim Is True' was released read as follows: (1) Barbra

Streisand (2) Johnny Mathis (3) The Muppets (4) Abba (5) Neil Diamond. The only remotely 'new wave' disc to sully the Top Ten was The Stranglers' debut sitting not-so-prettily at number 9. Elsewhere in the issue, *Melody Maker* ran their annual essay competition: first question "The new wave has nothing to do with music' – discuss…" On an adjacent page, staff writer/future editor Allan Jones launched what was to become a long-running love affair with Costello's music via a glowing review of the album, while to complete the picture Stiff ran a double page spread showing one-third of Elvis' less than beautiful body. "To collect your free dramatic action pic (sic) of Elvis, cut this out and stick it on the bedroom wall," it advised, noting that the other two-thirds could be purchased in *NME* and *Record Mirror*.

The publicity campaign was rumoured to be driving the label to the very verge of bankruptcy – but, as the album chart indicated, the impact of new artists and imaginative promotional ideas was hardly as far-reaching as retrospective histories have tended to infer. Yet with tour, album and adverts in the same issue, few readers could now pretend they hadn't heard of Elvis Costello – and they were soon going to hear a lot more.

Unbeknownst to most of the music press, The Attractions had already made their stage bow in a far-flung outpost of the rock circuit. They'd been sent away to rehearse in a cottage in Davidstowe, Cornwall, where they took the opportunity to play a short support set to 'transvestite punk' act Wayne County, at The Garden, a rock venue in nearby Penzance on 14 July. The gig was reportedly enlivened by an attempted stage invasion from The Damned's Captain Sensible who apparently wanted to jam with them. Emerging unscathed from the experience, they made their second live appearance at Woods Leisure Centre in Plymouth, picking up their first review from a *Record Mirror* stringer who described their performance as "machine-like…every song is rattled out effectively and efficiently." The intensive rehearsal sessions obviously paid quick dividends – and since money was tight, Costello and band showed their gratitude for the rent-free accommodation by promising to play the cottage owner's wedding in June the following year.

"If my friends could see me now," runs the famous song from 'Sweet Charity' – and with Costello's first utterances in the music-press came the suspicion that his Christian name might not have been *all* he'd been persuaded to change. Allan Jones of *Melody Maker*, who conducted the first in-depth interview with Elvis after having been mesmerised by his Nashville gig in May, recorded the complaint that, "Springsteen's always romanticising the fucking street…I'm bored with people who romanticise the fucking

street." Nor would he be drawn about his past: "If you weren't
there you missed it and that's it," he snarled in a broadside that was
to characterise his infrequent but bellicose utterances to the press
when he chose to make them. Jake Riviera, another music business
reject come good, was evidently encouraging him to vent his
bitterness and frustration at not being discovered one hell of a lot
sooner – and all the signs were that he was more than prepared to
indulge his manager's whim.

By the most unfortunate coincidence, the second of Elvis
Costello's rare interviews with the music press was published on 27
August 1977, eleven days after his rather more famous namesake
passed away: make of the symbolism what you will. The interview-
er was Nick Kent, *New Musical Express'* answer to Keith Richards
and something of a rock-writing legend in whom, it seemed, Elvis
found a kindred spirit. They made a strange pairing, the gangling,
vaguely untogether, leather clad Kent and the dapper, intense
Elvis: but time and again through the years to come Nick Kent
would be granted interviews when lesser mortals got no further
than the doorstep. In fact, for a long time, all the world knew of
Elvis Costello beyond what he chose to give away on vinyl filtered
out through Kent's pen.

On this occasion, Elvis took it into his head to utter some
highly quoteworthy quotes which rapidly became enshrined as part
of the man's myth. He also made clear his aversion to Island
Records, the larger independent label through which Stiff then
licensed their releases, principally because their A&R man Richard
Williams failed to recognise his potential. To give Williams his due
he wasn't the only one – yet Island was now eating its corporate
words as Costello made them money hand over clenched fist. It
was clear that Kent had been specially selected as spokesperson
for the man with the spectacles: indeed, he'd apparently already
appeared in 'Waiting For The End Of The World', as the 'man from
the television' who crawled into Costello's tube train one night on
the way home. But then again, that could have been *anyone-
…*couldn't it?

But while *New Musical Express* readers sat and pondered
whether Kent was having his ego fed, Jake Riviera was busy
elsewhere "hyping Elvis", as the sales campaign put it. Giving the
first thousand purchasers of the album the chance to have a free
copy sent to a friend was just one way in which the word was being
spread. *Real* success, though, meant reaching beyond the small
clique of music-press readers to the wide world beyond – and that
meant a hit single. The choice fell on 'Red Shoes', which looked to
succeed with a wry smile where the quirkiness of 'Less Than Zero'
and the undisguised emotion of 'Alison' had failed. Sadly it didn't –
and neither did a disastrous second-billing engagement to Santana

at the annual Crystal Palace Garden Party in September. From the clubs to an open-air stage in a matter of months was just too big a gap to bridge, as was the physical presence of Crystal Palace bowl's stagefront lake which stretched before him and a largely uncomprehending 15,000-strong audience. He stormed off, leaving a howl of feedback to express his feelings.

It was a rare mistake on Riviera's part during an inspired summer when even the publicity stunts that went wrong turned out right in the end. Being arrested in July outside the London Hilton Hotel for busking to CBS record executives *en route* to their annual convention could hardly be described as a stroke of luck; yet a £5 fine for obstruction was a small price to pay for front pages, radio reports and a full house for The Attractions' first ever London date at Dingwalls Dancehall that night. (Coincidence or not, CBS's parent company Columbia signed Costello for the US a few months later.) Full houses now became the rule rather than the exception, as the Nashville Rooms found in August when an estimated 1500 fans showed for Costello's appearance in the 400-capacity venue: Bonnie Raitt was among those locked out. The next four dates of a Sunday-night residency were promptly designated ticket-only, but that wasn't enough to save eight fans from being arrested for obstruction. It is not known whether Jake Riviera paid their £5 fines from the night's proceeds…

The success of 'My Aim Is True', which reached Number 4 in the British charts, enabled Flip City to realise their wildest dreams – albeit posthumously – when they made it onto vinyl at long last. Designed to resemble an official promotional album and even carrying the official 'Stiff' logo on a caricature of the original cover, 'Our Aim Is True' features the Flip City demo tape, all 9 tracks and 14 takes of it. Though many learned pop archivists have ascribed the backing to The Rumour or Clover, scrutiny of the song titles – 'Pay It Back', 'Living In Paradise', 'Radio Soul', 'Imagination' and 'Don't Stop The Band', along with covers of 'Knocking On Heaven's Door', 'Third Rate Romance', and 'I'm Packing Up' – revealed the truth behind the title.

Nick Lowe's solo career as an artist, meanwhile, was taking some unusual turns since 'So It Goes' and its follow-up EP 'Bowi', named because David Bowie 'mis-spelled' Nick's surname on *his* 'Low' album. He helped reclusive Welsh guitarist Dave Edmunds record a solo album, 'Get It', for the Swan Song label in 1977 and, after considerable behind-the-scenes effort from Jake Riviera who'd booked rehearsal rooms and generally chivvied things along, decided to make the union permanent. Rockpile, named after Edmunds' first solo album of the early Seventies, was a curious group – two writer producers in Edmunds and Lowe and a pair of extraordinarily talented backing musicians (if one dared call them that) in guitarist Billy Bremner and ex-Man/future Dire Straits drummer Terry Williams. The individuals' contractual situation was so complex that even Jake Riviera couldn't untangle it; while Lowe recorded for Radar, Edmunds' contract with Led Zeppelin's Swan Song meant that although the group gigged as Rockpile the albums came out under the name of the individual whose contract next stipulated a release.

The situation came to a head when prime mover and motivator Jake Riviera was abruptly replaced as Edmunds' manager by Zeppelin supremo Peter Grant, an equally dominant personality and a man with whom Lowe, for one, didn't see eye to eye. Both sides blamed each other for the split, but the writing was clearly on the wall. Rockpile was shipped to the States to support Swan Song megaband Bad Company, a 'dinosaur' rock group whose tour expenses alone could have run Stiff Records for a good year or so. Their replacement with only half the dates completed was, claimed Lowe, because, "In many of the next-day reviews we'd get a better write up than Bad Co…and rightly so. I mean they are about as exciting as a sack of old spuds."

The vegetables hit the fan a short while later with Lowe's departure, announcing that working with Edmunds was "too restrictive" and talking about a new line-up with ex-Pink Fairy Larry Wallis. The experience inspired Costello to write a song, 'Hand In Hand', as a warning of the rock-star mentality that he felt typified the Led Zeppelin/Swan Song operation. "The main figure…is the sort of inhuman monster type I could become if I let myself go *that* far," commented Costello, making it clear elsewhere that Jimmy Page was the person in question. Meanwhile, Lowe had his own album to do – until, that was, he received a phone-call one sunny day in June…

It was the summer of punk, or so the history books tell us. And Jubilee Day brought the symbolic clash (no pun intended) between the generations. As the Queen celebrated 25 years of rule over her green and pleasant land, The Sex Pistols were engaged in a riverboat cruise on the River Thames to commemorate the chart success of their less-than-reverent anthem, 'God Save The Queen'. As police launches swarmed around the Pistols' boat like enraged bees, Costello called Nick Lowe to demand his attention. He'd written a new song that had to be recorded - *now*. Pausing only to call up The Rumour's rhythm section of Andrew Bodnar and Steve Goulding, Lowe headed for Pathway Studios. The result of this spontaneous recording session was 'Watching The Detectives', a track which fully eight years later stands acknowledged as one of Costello's greatest.

Reggae's rebel music was taken up by punks as providing a

parallel to their own sounds and an alternative to the sanitised commercial pop they so despised. It wasn't long before the off-beat 'rydims' of Jamaica crossed over into the musical mainstream of new-wave via The Clash, whose version of Lee Perry's 'Police And Thieves' was included on their debut album released in April. Costello later admitted that 'Watching The Detectives' was inspired by The Clash's reggaematic rock: certainly it wasn't an influence his music had previously exhibited.

As Bodnar and Goulding laid down a dense, brooding offbeat, Elvis scattered shards of splintering, reverbed guitar across the bleakest of aural landscapes. The lyrics carelessly mix fantasy with reality: a cop show on the television watched by a couple in their front room suddenly lurches into real-life with a horrifying inevitability. Costello whispers, snarls, observes and chills, his repetition on the 'shoot, shoot, shoot, SHOOT' sequence emphasizing one of his most effective and scary vocal techniques. The American album was re-mastered to include 'Detectives', and no wonder – this was one of the sounds 1977 would be best remembered for.

'Watching The Detectives' was to be Stiff's twentieth single: BUY 20 in the jokey matrix-number series that started with Nick Lowe's self-explanatory BUY 1. But despite the critical plaudits, the Great British public simply weren't BUYing enough for Stiff to survive and thrive. Accordingly, Jake Riviera resurrected a brainwave of two years earlier – the Naughty Rhythms Tour. Remember the formula? Package a number of bands, rotate the running order and present them at various downmarket venues nationwide at a low ticket price. He'd backed the wrong horse back in 1975 – but this time round, all five runners were Stiffs. And that sounded like good odds…

Costello's running-mates on the tour provided a variety of sights and sounds under the Stiff Records banner. The 'form horse' was Ian Dury, once of Kilburn and the High Roads and now backed by The Blockheads, a seven-piece band whose musical muscle rivalled even The Attractions. Nick Lowe and Dave Edmunds patched things up enough to form (with Terry Williams) the basis of the fluctuating line-up of Lowe's quaintly-named Last Chicken In The Shop, while ex-Pink Fairy Larry Wallis used most of the same personnel to back him as The Psychedelic Rowdies. Last and very possibly least came the previously mentioned Wreckless Eric, whose defiantly uncommercial ditties lent themselves to backing by Blockhead sax-player Davey Payne, Ian Dury on drums and Dury's girlfriend Denise Roudette on bass.

Opening at High Wycombe Town Hall on 3 October, the tour was to take in no fewer than 24 venues in a calendar month. As the 'Bunch of Stiffs' wound their way through the town halls and seats of learning of Merrie England, 'Watching The Detectives' was busy ascending the lower reaches of the singles chart, breaking into the Top Twenty in November and peaking at Number 15. But all was not well with Stiff. As Elvis' reputation and popularity grew, so Jake Riviera was reported to be becoming disillusioned with the day-to-day running of the record company. "It was doing his head in," commented general manager/associate Paul Conroy. In addition to their half shares in the record label, Riviera and Robinson also had the careers of Graham Parker, The Rumour, Nick Lowe, Clover and The Damned to concern themselves with under the Advance-dale Management banner. Costello was clearly on the way to becoming a big fish; it was time to take him to a somewhat less crowded pool.

Meanwhile the tour went on, its madness fuelled the more by rumours of impending events. The music papers vied to cover the package in the most lurid detail, encouraging such bizarre practices as the '24-Hour Club', a fraternity of musicians and others led by Dave Edumunds and Jarry Wallis who apparently existed without sleep. Edmunds and Nick Lowe fell out again, the Welsh-man leaving the tour at Manchester only to return without comment a little further along the way. There were also the more conventional problems encountered by touring musicians such as Wreckless Eric's laryngitis, which also struck at Manchester. On this occasion extended sets from both The Attractions and Block-heads saved the day, Costello's impromptu rendition of Eric's 'Whole Wide World' acknowledging the absence of his sickly label-mate.

Such tales of cameraderie, high jinks and pioneering spirit are, so they say, the stuff of which rock legends are made. As far as Costello was concerned, though, the Stiff tour was to be an experi-ence he would rather forget. He dissociated himself from the various excesses which such communal living tends to encourage, remaining true to his public image by sinking down into the seat of the touring bus in wraparound dark glasses and refusing to social-ise. If the tour's theme song, Ian Dury's 'Sex And Drugs And Rock And Roll', was beginning to ring rather too true for certain mem-bers of the Stiff crew, then it was symbolic that though Elvis dutifully reappeared to take part in the massed encore chorus of the said anthem, video film tends to support the contention that his contribution was *mimed*... In the short term, the tour probably didn't have too much of a promotional impact on the sales of 'Watching The Detectives', which was getting enough airplay to chart anyway; in the long term, it inspired an 'answer song', if you like, to 'Sex And Drugs' in 'Pump It Up', which was to appear on Elvis' next album.

Costello and Lowe were each obliged by the terms of their

contract to make one more record for Stiff. In Costello's case it was 'Detectives', released on 14 October and backed with two live cuts recorded at the Nashville on 7 August – 'Blame It On Cain' and a pulsating 'Mystery Dance' – while the wily Lowe threw away a cover version. 'Halfway To Paradise' was a Goffin-King Brill Building classic that Billy Fury had taken to the UK Top Ten in 1961.

Nick and Elvis also contributed a brace of tracks apiece to the 'Stiffs Live' album that emerged from the tour. While Lowe's tracks were loud 'n' obnoxious pub-rock rave-ups, Costello added at least one largely unrecognised jewel to his crown in resurrecting Bacharach and David's 'I Just Don't Know What To Do With Myself'. Some years later he was to repay his loan from Dusty Springfield's repertoire with a self-penned number entitled 'Just A Memory'; for now, the emotion that stretched his voice almost to breaking point and stilled the madding college crowd was rather more than memorable. 'Miracle Man' made up the Costello quota and was the second live version to surface, a London-recorded cut from the same Nashville gig as the 'Detectives' live cuts that already appeared on the US flip of 'Alison'. Stiff's promotional ads for the album – with pictures of Lowe and Costello – still ran defiantly as the two started their recording careers elsewhere, yet while the album itself is now little more than a dusty 'you should have been there' souvenir, Costello's classic cover will always make the search for a copy worthwhile.

Round about this time, a rumour spread to the effect that Elvis had once been a founder-member of The Sex Pistols, of all people. As it turned out, the seed was sown by *ZigZag* author, artist and archivist Pete Frame who was wont to insert certain practical jokes into his famous family trees in order to see how many times they were picked up and repeated by other writers. His 'Children of the Revolution' chart mischievously suggested Costello might have been the mysterious Wally who'd played guitar in an embryo Sex Pistols line-up known as The Swankers. *Time Out* picked up the story, ironically in view of their Flip City connections, but dropped it hurriedly after Frame admitted his misdemeanour. Still, any publicity was good publicity, it seemed – and a future by-product of this secrecy game was the formation in 1979 of the Elvis Costello Information Service, a magazine run by fanatics that exists to this day exchanging news, reviews and trivia of every description.

Back in 1977, though, the first priority for Jake Riviera was to break his charge in America, where 'My Aim Is True' had already distinguished itself by becoming the biggest import album in history. (It eventually reached Number 32 four months after its release by Columbia.) But a record, when bought, becomes the property of its owner, to be played and replayed at will. The

American press and publicity machine, much to its chagrin, was
soon to discover that the same was not true of Elvis Costello the
performer. With a vengeful Riviera pulling the strings, Costello was
quick to cut through the cool exterior of the US media.

An invitation to play two live numbers in the coast-to-coast
TV show 'Saturday Night Live' brought an unexpected response;
after plugging the recently released 'Watching The Detectives',
Costello and The Attractions were scheduled to play 'Less Than
Zero', but as far as its author was concerned it had been "written
about an English situation and didn't really fit". With a curt "I'm
sorry ladies and gentlemen, there's no reason to do this song," he
aborted in mid-introduction. Perceptive viewers might have recalled that The Attractions were appearing in place of The Sex Pistols,
who were in the process of disintegrating along with their American
tour; Bruce Thomas even wore a 'Thanks Malc' T-shirt.

But there was little warning of the fact that an unreleased,
uncensored and therefore totally unsuitable song was about to be
unleashed on an unsuspecting American public. The blisteringly
scornful 'Radio Radio' that beamed its way loud and clear into
millions of homes across the continent found a poor reception in the
TV studios, where it was made clear that the invitation was unlikely
to be repeated. It was to be February 1981 before US television
dared screen Elvis live again.

The seeds were sown for a love-hate relationship with the
US press that was to have unfortunate repercussions further down
the line. Costello needed to sell records but was unwilling to sell
himself – and unlike in his own country, where a cult figure could
find some measure of fame through the power of the press, US
radio and television held all the aces. It was a dangerous game, and
the opening hand had just been played; for now, though, everything
in the garden was just rosy. Costello had every right to look back on
the past year through those big black-rimmed glasses with a smile.

This Year's Elvis

If 'Watching The Detectives' brought 1977 to a spectacular and wholly satisfactory close, there was no question of any complacency setting in: what to many of the year's punk bands would have been success beyond their wildest dreams was just the first step in Jake Riviera's master plan. By the time Costello returned to Blighty to play a three-day Christmas Eve residency at the same Nashville Rooms he'd graced as a solo act in May, the ink had dried on the label on which his next release would appear.

Radar Records combined the talents of Jake Riviera, United Artists' former managing director Martin Davis, and that same label's erstwhile A&R chief Andrew Lauder. UA had many connections with the Stiff clan, having signed the Brinsleys and Feelgoods among others. Andrew Lauder saw Radar emulating Stiff and Chiswick, labels run "by fans who not only wanted to do it themselves but were able to do it with the right attitude...", pointing out that Radar could do likewise "because we have even more experience and expertise". Loading the dice in their favour, of course, was their signing (for the world excluding the US, Canada and Scandinavia) of Costello and Lowe, both now seemingly commercial certainties. Weighing against Radar, however, was the label's reliance on funding from the giant WEA (Warner, Elektra, Atlantic) conglomerate which, although it didn't much influence everyday decisions, was to have far-reaching consequences a couple of years down the road.

Meanwhile, the green light shone for Elvis and his Attractions, who undertook a second stint along the freeways of America in their Greyhound bus, playing a number of dates as guests of Talking Heads. It was a fascinating contrast: the anorexic, angst ridden David Byrne and his stripped-down backing band against a bespectacled, uncompromising Costello fronting the supercharged Attractions; a psychotic package indeed. As if to prove that his antipathy to the press knew no national boundaries, he gave only two short interviews in the six weeks they were there.

The tour started in New Orleans on 26 January – and by the time The Attractions reached Toronto, their final port of call, on 6 March they were fairly steaming. Local radio station CHUM-FM was broadcasting live from the El Mocambo, a sweaty little 500-capacity club in which The Rolling Stones recorded a side of their 'Love You Live' album not a year previously – Keith Richard's trial on drugs offences relating to that visit was still to come. With 1000 people turned away at the door (Margaret Trudeau, sadly, didn't show this time) Toronto seemed hooked on Costello; and with a similar two-night residency in prospect, it seemed logical for Columbia Records to record the gigs. The result was 'Live At The El Mocambo', originally pressed in a limited edition of 500 for release to US radio stations but since much bootlegged.

From Jake Riviera's point of view it wasn't particularly desirable to have live versions of currently unreleased material on the airwaves or making money for bootleggers: this wasn't his first (and certainly not his last) difference of opinion with Costello's US label. But the record deserves its legendary status for capturing Elvis and band at their most aggressive and muscular, despite a few bum notes from the man with the guitar. And anyone who can raise a cheer with the words "We've come to ask for the country back" had to be doing *something* right…

Elvis and The Attractions warmed up for this tour, their first major Stateside exposure, with a free gig at London's Roundhouse on 20 January where they were supported by Whirlwind and The Soft Boys. The fuel for Elvis and The Attractions' rocketing reputation as a live act was provided in almost equal measure by songs from 'My Aim Is True', and material destined for their yet-to-be recorded follow-up. Playing half a set of unknown material would have been enough for most bands to handle, but even more fascinating was The Attractions' approach to the older songs. One or two – 'Welcome To The Working Week' and 'Red Shoes' for instance – stayed true to their recorded versions, more or less, but the majority of survivors took on a new life.

'Waiting For The End Of The World' was a case in point. A fearsomely apocalyptic vision sprung from nowhere, it made the album version sound positively polite from Costello's very first imitation Sex Pistol guitar riff. Nieve forsook his customary stabbing organ style for some swirling Ray Manzarek-style fills, piling on the pressure and inspiring Elvis to harangue the unsuspecting spectators as if the very spirit of Jim Morrison was wracking his puny body. "I been waiting…for so long. For *soooooo* long."he gasped as if his – and everybody else's – life depended on it. The consequences were nothing less than frightening.

'Less Than Zero' was another 'Aim' number to undergo major surgery – this time at its writer's instigation. It wasn't a number that travelled well – Sir Oswald Mosley, the Fascist Party leader whose television appearance inspired the song, was hardly a household name in 1977 Britain, let alone on more distant shores. So when Elvis realised that American audiences connected 'Mr. Oswald with the swastika tattoo' with Lee Harvey Oswald, John F. Kennedy's assassin, he adjusted his sights accordingly – and Less Than Zero's Dallas version was the result. If anything, this alternative scenario was even more fraught than its predecessor, and certainly more explicit.

The long-awaited second album was unveiled in March – and from the cover to the runoff groove it was a distinctly disorientating proposition. The visuals were instantly arresting – Costello behind a tripod-mounted camera, with both image and titles deliberately off-centre, backed by a 'What's wrong with this picture?' (or was it a double exposure?) of the band in a motel room, the likes of which they'd seen a lot of by now. The inner bag was no more illuminating – a gloved hand held a miniature television (with Elvis on screen, naturally), while four variously-coloured clothes-shop dummies in a launderette adorned the reverse. But it was the music inside which ultimately drew the greater attention.

Despite the sleeve's lack of a band credit, the label's announcement of 'Elvis Costello and The Attractions' was both timely and appropriate. For this was a *band* album, without a doubt, and as such an enormous progression from 'My Aim Is True'. Twelve songs made their point with conviction and economy: *Sounds'* Jon Savage compared it with the Stones' 'Aftermath' in "its accuracy in pinpointing targets and hitting them", while Nick Kent in *NME* equated the album's relationship with its predecessor to the Band's 'Big Pink' and 'The Band'. For those whose musical memories don't extend back quite *that* far, Kent's concluding epithet – "uneasy listening" – gives a more universally understandable verdict on a landmark album.

However it may have been marketed, 'My Aim Is True' bore the unmistakable stamp of a singer-songwriter. Given they had only been together for six months, was it reasonable to expect anything different from the new team of Costello and The Attractions on their follow-up? The answer is yes – and no. On the plus side, the great majority of the songs on 'This Year's Model' were already staples of The Attractions' live set, while the many years of studio experience behind the Thomases and producer Nick Lowe provided numerous permutations and possibilities in terms of recording. Then again, though, the players' collective confidence wasn't always strong enough to withstand Nick Lowe's encouragement of some wholesale pop plundering which saw many Sixties licks re-upholstered for a Seventies audience. But no amount of criticism can obscure the fact that 'This Year's Model' possessed an excitement, a vitality, a spark that its predecessor had only been able to hint at. One distinguished commentator pinpointed the difference between the two albums as "description" and "definition"; observation and involvement came to mind as being equally appropriate adjectives. 'This Year's Model' was the kind of album to leave any listener drained.

Musically, the reference points veered wildly from Merseybeat to glam, with snatches of melody that nagged at the listener's memory long after the record deck had ceased spinning. On a song like 'This Year's Girl', an indictment of the fashion-following *femme* described by its author as "a female 'Miracle Man'", the Ringo Starr backbeat and steadily-building middle eight recalled nothing so much as some Frankenstein-like mutation of 'You Can't Do That'. There were two definite differences, though; one was Steve Nieve's piping, garage-band organ, the second Costello's lyrics. Words and phrases leapt into sharp relief like red ink from a page. Subversive pop – or what?

Surprisingly, given the success of 'Watching The Detectives' and its sinister reggae undertow, there was little on 'This Year's Model' to suggest a continuing love affair with the off-beat. The closest approximation came with '(I Don't Want To Go To) Chelsea', a lurching litany of obscure film references ; *Smashing Time*, a 1967 cult movie, and Antonioni's better-known psychedelic epic *Blow Up* providing the grist to Costello's lyric mill. He later described the song as being "like snapshots intercut between two movies", but Columbia evidently considered its terms of reference too British for the American pressing of the album.

Completing the trilogy of anti-fashion anthems with 'This Year's Girl' and 'Chelsea' was 'Lipstick Vogue', one of the live set's most powerful songs which revolved around Pete Thomas' thunderous drums. With scarcely a solo of any kind on the album, it might seem contrary to liken Thomas' performance to Keith Moon of The Who's tendency to solo through every song, yet what was necessarily lost in raw power through the translation to vinyl was cleverly countered by a mid-song lull, the calm before a veritable storm of percussive energy and a refinement which, like other studio-inspired modifications through the album, was to be duplicated in the live performances that followed.

If certain aspects of 'This Year's Model' were undeniably borrowed, there was one old song among the new and not so new. 'Living In Paradise' had been a regular in the Flip City repertoire during 1975 – indeed, a pre-Stiff Dave Robinson had been known to request it from the back of the Red Cow bar during the band's last weeks. Costello claims it was also cut for the 'Aim' sessions, which may or may not be a smokescreen to hide its origins. The fact that its wordplay isn't quite up to Elvis' usual slick standards marks it down as an older song: a vision of a rock'n'roll Babylon that must have seemed a lot closer to Costello now than when he originally wrote it.

'Lip Service', a number with obvious on-stage dedication possibilities fully exploited by Elvis (especially in the direction of Island Records executives), combined both menace and melody in its put down of authority in general – and A&R men in particular. Rejection was clearly something he wouldn't take lying down. 'You wanna throw me away/But I'm not broken' ran a line in 'Lipstick Vogue' from a man clearly obsessed with survival at a time when punk bands were biting the dust faster than torn bin-liners.

'Pump It Up' chronicled the Stiff tour in so many words, matching its diatribe to a relentless riffing from organ and bass. The song basically boasted two chords and two chords only; the hoped-for relief provided by a third chord never came, leaving the listener – as Costello intended – unsatisfied and unfulfilled. Offspring of Dylan's 'Subterranean Homesick Blues' it might have been, yet Zimmerman himself couldn't have pulled a neater musical tease than *that*... And even the less obvious songs had a message: from starting with a line swiped from Cliff Richard's 'Summer Holiday', 'The Beat' turns into something rather more sinister. 'I don't wanna be a lover/I just wanna be your victim', must be Costello's most quoted line, yet it was one which laid out his stall in the emotional cattle-market with startling clarity.

Even the superficially happy songs were shot through with a certain cynicism. Take the best Small Faces song Steve Marriott never wrote, 'You Belong To Me'; it sounds jolly enough until you realise the singer's saying 'no' instead of 'yes'. As with all Costello's most interesting songs, though, the listener is hooked and happily singing the chorus before he or she gets down to listening to the verse. Interestingly the song hadn't been intended for the album at all, having been commissioned by Nick Lowe for Dr. Feelgood. Studio sources had it that Lee Brilleaux found the lyrics "a bit war'n'peace" and that the take, intended for the Lowe-produced 'Be Seeing You' sessions, was then abandoned. Its inclusion, together with the years-old 'Living In Paradise', may have indicated the pressure Costello was under to produce new material – yet both songs provided welcome relief from the musical intensity around them. And besides, could a man who claimed he had "400 songs under wraps" *ever* run out of new material completely?

If the majority of these short, superficially poppy songs were invested with a new menace live, then perhaps 'Night Rally', the album's parting shot, came closer than most to reproducing that quality on disc. Omitted on the American pressing in favour of the more universal sentiments of 'Radio Radio', it combined the bleaker aspects of 'Less Than Zero's' cautionary anti-Fascist message with the fatalism of 'Waiting For The End Of The World' (the song it currently followed to end the live set) to end the album on an explicit and disturbingly pessimistic note.

Like 'My Aim Is True', 'This Year's Model' could almost fit comfortably onto one side of a C-60 cassette – no bad thing perhaps, given that the similarities between some of the arrangements suggest that the musical cards held by Lowe and Costello could only be shuffled a finite number of ways. Yet unlike its predecessor, which Costello later dismissively described as "just a collection of songs", 'Model' was an album that provoked and involved the listener as much as it entertained. Given the emotional spectrum packed into the grooves, it's a wonder the Bible Belt didn't examine it for Satanic messages playing backwards somewhere amid theNick Lowe production.

And Lowe proved equal to the job of distilling the power of The Attractions' performances onto vinyl. Having flown over to New York for the mastering process of transferring tape to record, he apparently surprised the cutting engineer by declining to indicate the volumes and frequency boosting usually required during mastering to give the record those all-important added dynamics. "It's all right," laughed Lowe as he left. "Just bash it down and make it as loud as possible." The result speaks for itself.

The choice of 45 fcll on '(I Don't Want To Go To) Chelsea', released a week prior to the album as part of Radar's first singles salvo along with Nick Lowe's 'I Love The Sound Of Breaking Glass' and Iggy Pop/James Williamson's 'Kill City' – and though the world still wasn't ready for the Godfather of Punk, 'Chelsea' and 'Breaking Glass' both reached the Top Twenty to make Numbers 16 and 7 respectively. And if it was disappointing for Elvis to have faltered one place short of 'Detectives' – let alone be pipped by his producer – there was solace in the fact that 'This Year's Model', even without the benefit of the Stiff advertising tactics enjoyed by its predecessor, soared to Number 4.

The month-long British tour that started, perversely, in the Irish capital of Dublin on 16 March and wound up with two nights at the Roundhouse in London on 15-16 April, gave home-based fans their first taste of the album in its entirety; although most of the songs – 'Lip Service', 'Pump It Up', 'The Beat' and 'Night Rally' among others – had been in the repertoire for some while, they were probably more familiar to American audiences. And there was more to come, as Elvis continued to perform cover versions. Audiences at various points in the tour could expect to hear one or more from The Damned's 'Neat Neat Neat', Ian Dury's 'Roadette Song', Richard Hell's 'Love Comes In Spurts' and John Sebastian's 'Six O'Clock' among the self-composed selections. 'Neat' had already appeared on the flip of the 'Stranger In The House' freebie given away to early buyers of 'This Year's Model', while Richard Hell was soon to become a Radar favourite alongside Costello himself.

The British tour (on which The Attractions were supported by Mickey Jupp) didn't lack its quota of drama, especially when Bruce Thomas badly injured his hand opening a beer bottle in Manchester. Luckily, Elvis knew a bass-player who was more than familiar with the new album and was prepared to step in at a moment's notice – take a bow Nicholas Lowe. By the end of the tour competition developed for the guest bass player's slot. Thin Lizzy's Phil Lynott took his revenge for Lowe's flattering imitation of his group on 'So It Goes' to try his hand. One of the band's final London dates with Lowe as their deputy bass player was recorded on the aptly-titled 'Accidents' bootleg.

If Elvis' choice of covers betrayed his eclectic musical taste, then his guest appearance on Capital Radio's 'Your Mother Wouldn't Like It' shortly after his return from the States went some way further. Some years later he was to state, "What I enjoy most on days off is to go to radio stations and do DJ shows, because I think you give away more of what you're about." Elvis' personal selection of singles included tracks by Fleetwood Mac, Bob Dylan, T. Rex, George Jones, Graham Parsons and Bowie – a mixed bunch indeed.

If, as Costello suggests, "You give away what makes your music tick the same way as you go to somebody's house and look at the bookshelf," that list may speak volumes. Whatever, it was the first sign of a certain sociability. And, with Elvis' departure for yet another US tour, a record was what British fans were left with – or more specifically 'Pump It Up', – familiar to his audience as the set closer as well as an album track. The B-side was a new cut, 'Big Tears', which featured Clash guitarist Mick Jones augmenting The Attractions. Though Jones was not greatly in evidence, there was a general feeling that the track deserved more than to be the flip-side of a number 24 single.

Radar/Riviera had a double stake in Costello's third Stateside sojourn, for the package tour he headed included Nick Lowe on a bill made up by Mink De Ville, a combo that scored a hit in 1977 with 'Spanish Stroll' but found the commercial going tough thereafter. Their leader, Willy De Ville, reckoned himself pretty tough, too, and let it be known in interviews that he didn't much fancy this rum looking Englishman using the name of the great Elvis. His roadies didn't get on with The Attractions' crew either, and the matter was settled in customary rough-house fashion.

Columbia Records, on whose label Lowe and Costello both appeared that side of the Atlantic, issued an EP of the three package artists in clear orange vinyl – and such was Costello's

popularity that the disc was soon bootlegged. The album, meanwhile, reached number 30 – an all-important two places better than
its predecessor and the first 'new wave' LP to achieve such giddy
heights. Another barometer of public opinion was the $20 that touts
outside the sold-out 3000-seater Santa Monica Civic were asking
for $10 tickets. If Elvis' street value had doubled, his audience had
multiplied sixfold – last time in town he'd been playing to less than
500 souls at the Whisky.

His 20-song set for this marathon 10-week tour showed
changes, too, from his previous visit. New arrivals included the set
closer 'Final Solution' (destined to turn up on his next album retitled
'Chemistry Class') and a song that could be described as the
antithesis of every paean to the power of rock 'n' roll radio ever
crooned in three-part harmony to catch the self-worshipping DJ's
ear. Equalled only in cynicism by Neil Young's 1983 'Payola Blues',
it was 'Radio Radio'.

Bar-poppers at the Red Cow, Hammersmith in November
1975 alongside Dave Robinson would have found 'Radio Radio'
quite familar – until they listened to the words. For while Flip City's
lead singer had believed in the 'Radio Soul' and its "sound salva-
tion", his hornrimmed descendant felt nothing but anger and bet-
rayal. "I wanna bite the hand that feeds me…so badly." howled
Costello in what *NME's* Tony Parsons once memorably termed his
"Angry Young Man Whine".

Unlike Lou Reed's 'Walk On The Wild Side' or, later, Frank-
ie Goes To Hollywood's 'Relax', there was to be no subversive,
secret seduction here. Although Radio 1's Paul Gambaccini bravely
put his neck on the chopping block by making 'Radio Radio' his
record of the week, his reaction was exceptional rather than the
rule. The same station's asinine 'housewives' choice', Tony Black-
burn, insisted that Elvis was a "silly little man" every time the
playlist compelled him to introduce the disc, and he habitually
dissociated himself from the lyrical content. Costello got a chance
to avenge himself when invited to perform on BBC-TV's 'Top Of
The Pops' chart show. Instead of indicting 'such a lot of fools' who
control the airwaves, he slyly changed the lyric to read 'silly little
men', waving contemptuously at the compère – yes, Tony Black-
burn – as the pre-recorded track played through behind him. "Ah,
we mustn't take these things personally," blustered the embarrassed DJ as he gingerly advanced within camera range once more.

Though 'Radio Radio' had bags more commercial appeal
than, say, The Clash's 'Capital Radio', that didn't mean it would get
airplay – and so it proved. No surprise, then, when it continued
Costello's downwards singles slide from 'Detectives' number 15
through 16 and 24 to number 29 – hanging on to the Thirty for grim
life.

'Radio Radio' entered the charts in late October 1978, just as the second Stiff Tour set off on a repeat journey around the UK. All its passengers – Lene Lovich, Mickey Jupp, Rachel Sweet and Jona Lewie – were new arrivals; only poor Wreckless Eric remained from the first tour, his record sales having signally failed to pay his fare. In all respects, the second tour was a pale imitation of the trailblazing enterprise in which Costello had participated. Nevertheless, Radar Records' own end of term report had not been as encouraging as all that. Costello and Lowe remained the principal acts; few other artists of note were added to the roster, while an attempt to sign The Tourists (with future Eurythmics Annie Lennox and Dave Stewart) was destined to fall through. All efforts had been concentrated on breaking Costello (and, to a lesser degree, Lowe) in the States. Would the gamble pay off?

In contrast to many pop stars then and now, Costello always made a point of keeping his private life under wraps, claiming to be "very, very 'country music' in my attitude" to talking about such affairs. And besides, with Rod Stewart and his ilk gadding about with sundry leggy blondes, what would the newspapers want to know about a regular husband and father with a house in suburban Middlesex?

So when Elvis was spotted at an open-air concert in Hyde Park by punk poet John Cooper Clarke one Sunday in late October it came as a shock to find his companion was glamorous model Bebe Buell, previously a close friend of Todd Rundgren and…Rod Stewart. Though Costello tried to avoid this first sighting by pulling his pork-pie hat down over his face, he surely must have known the news would spread, and shortly afterwards it was confirmed that he'd moved out of his marital home to a Kensington flat to continue a relationship that seemed so completely out of character as to be disturbing.

As the singer's devoted fans watched and worried about the significance of *his* devotion, Elvis and The Attractions dodged out of the country to complete the year's globetrotting with dates in Canada, Hawaii, Japan and Australia. In Japan, where 'My Aim Is True' had just been belatedly released, The Attractions' promotional tactic of playing on an open truck saw Elvis pick up his second busking fine but find an enthusiastic new audience; not only was new wave unknown in the land of the Rising Sun, but the Japanese were unused to foreign bands playing in small clubs in preference to large auditoriums like the Budokan.

After the past year's concentration on reaching the world's record markets, Jake Riviera was well aware that Elvis had become some kind of musical exile. Regardless of what part this constant touring may or may not have played in disrupting the singer's domestic life, it was clearly time to see whether an absence from home shores had made his audience's heart grow fonder. Would this stranger, we wondered, return to packed houses?

Armed And Dangerous

As 1978 ended, the stage was well and truly set for the commer-
cialisation of Elvis Costello. With no fewer than seven consecutive
nights inked in at London's Dominion Theatre, he was matching a
precedent set only by Judy Garland way back when and screamy-
bop star David Essex somewhat more recently. What was more,
the cinematic production he was so rudely elbowing aside was none
other than the blockbusting 'Star Wars'. But if the 'sold out' signs
spelled success, reports of unsavoury incidents from abroad
advised caution. Reading between the lines, it seemed that Costello was no Luke Skywalker – and what price Jake in the Darth Vader
mask?

The *NME* reported a recent backstage fracas in foreign
parts between Costello, Riviera and cameraman Richard Wood
who, by a wicked chance, just happened to be ace writer Tony
Parsons' not so long lost cousin. An *agent provocateur*? Perhaps.
But there came corroborated reports from Australia of "Angry
Punk Rock Fans On The Rampage". Even allowing for colonial
hyperbole, reports of a 50-minute set suggested that Costello had
all but played himself out. Not so his Aussie audience who, enraged
by announcements of tickets being available for the fourth of a
scheduled five shows and their inability to summon the band from
their dressing room, let fly with Fosters cans, seats and anything
else to hand.

The portents seemed ominous, then, when Costello went in
to bat at the Dominion. The choice of support, too, tended to pull
the rug from under the populist audience he must have realised his
seven-night residency would attract. First off, stand-up poet/comic
John Cooper Clarke rattled off his incomprehensible Mancunian
doggerel to a bemused reception, then Richard Hell, the original
punk whose ideas so impressed Malcolm McLaren four years
previously, took the stage. The reaction was predictable. In the
words of Nigel Cross, editor/publisher of *Bucketful Of Brains*
fanzine, "The audience reacted like stuffed dummies…I loved it,

but the poseurs all headed for the bar."

The stage was set, then, for Elvis to poop the party – and this he solemnly proceeded to do. In commercial terms, the objective was to preview his upcoming album, tentatively titled 'Emotional Fascism'. Instead, the performance – not an overly long one at that – seemed more tired than emotional. In Nigel Cross' words, again, it was, "a set that sounded tired, sterile and boring…I left before the end". Even those who remained seemed mixed in their response, despite the palliative of a free single of two songs in the set, 'Wednesday Week' and 'Talking In The Dark'. Elvis even broke off the intro of 'Watching The Detectives' to berate their lack of enthusiasm.

Two letters from the *New Musical Express* mailbag the following week responded directly to Costello's comments. "I must apologise," read the first, "to Elvis Costello for the appalling behaviour of the audience…we were so ungrateful, we took the free records and badges, we bought the T-shirts and programmes but we didn't go mad when you hit the stage." The second letter was rather more hard-hitting. "Listen, myopic one," it declared, "The Ramones, The Undertones and The Rezillos don't need to tell me to dance – why should you?"

Of course, the plush, upmarket Dominion was hardly a place where dancing in the aisles was encouraged; these were the first and last shows Costello was to play at the cinema venue until 1984. But the fact remained that with seven nights at a 1,975-seat venue, Elvis was reaching nearly 14,000 fans or potential fans, and this fact alone made his lacklustre performances all the more disappointing. 'What's So Funny 'Bout Peace Love And Understanding' ran the song The Attractions inherited from Brinsley Schwarz as a stage anthem (and incidentally, released unannounced as the B-side of composer Nick Lowe's 'American Squirm' the previous October). For one reason or another, the Dominion shows inspired none of these virtues.

If Elvis was spreading his talents somewhat thinly in live performance, his third album released in February 1979 was as calculated a piece of pop as was to appear in that – or any other year. 'Emotional Fascism' had disappeared as the title and the album was released as 'Armed Forces' at Pete Thomas' suggestion; the punning link was clearly nothing less than deliberate. Once again it was the packaging that beguiled and intrigued the casual buyer who, if he or she was quick enough off the mark, found among the origami of the fold-out cover a bonus seven-inch EP. Recorded at Hollywood High School on 4 June 1978, it featured three live tracks: an extended 'Watching The Detectives', a typically passionate 'Alison' and a piano-and-vocal rendition of the album's 'Accidents Will Happen' that for impact and intensity outscored the studio cut in every way.

But this was a distraction, however welcome, from the main event – or should it be the main course? 'Armed Forces' took Costello's staple subject matter and sugared the pill, coating his concerns with a pure-pop sheen that producer Nick Lowe had previously proved himself adept at applying to his own work. It was clear that 'Radio Radio' belonged firmly in the 'This Year's Model' section of the Costello canon; his "Angry Young Man Whine" had now matured into vintage pop that made his rivals taste like so much plonk.

'Oliver's Army' was the appetiser. Released as a single in January, it encapsulated the musical slant of 'Armed Forces' in a nutshell – multi-tracked vocals chiming in at frequent intervals, a strong melody and, more than anything, a catchy, addictive chorus that people found themselves singing first and thinking about afterwards. The lyrics related very much to the album's title, detailing the adventures of a reluctant mercenary who would "rather be anywhere else than here today", yet were married to a tune of anthemic proportions. Strangely enough, the song had very nearly failed to make the album at all; until Steve added his exuberant piano part, a close relation to Abba's 'Dancing Queen' riff, Costello considered it a non-starter. As it was, it became Elvis' most successful single, heavy radio play taking it to number 2, trailering the album in fine style.

The piano, so dominant on the single, was far from the main ingredient elsewhere on the album; the overall sound was sweetly synthesised, with traditional keyboard sounds at a premium. Take 'Green Shirt', a bubbling, pulsing fusion of Pete Thomas' military snare-drum, Costello's insistent, almost spoken vocal and a considerable amount of Steve Nieve on everything but the kitchen sink. Inspired by haughty British newscaster Angela Rippon, it was the latest in a lengthening line of songs relating to the media, but the sinister implications of the music for once scarcely seemed matched by lyrics which failed to live up to the promise of the opening couplet. Just as dancing seemed synonymous with sex on the first album, 'Armed Forces' boasted its own loose theme: the premise that love and war were one and the same thing. This was scarcely an earthshatteringly original idea, and presumbably the only excuse for including 'Goon Squad', the nearest Costello ever came to heavy metal with an intro straight out of the Thin Lizzy songbook and a string of military clichés that couldn't put up much of a fight against such a musical barrage.

In March of the previous year, Costello told Nick Kent he'd written a song for Ian Dury: nigh on twelve months later, it inexplicably surfaced on side two of 'Armed Forces'. Lurching along in 6/4 time, a grotesque parody of Dury's stumbling gait, 'Sunday's Best' really made little sense in the context of a Costello album and was fittingly dropped on the American release in favour of 'Peace Love And Understanding'.

'Chemistry Class' was another song that had been around for some while – and while its venomous, brooding concert performances (often ending the set on a spine-chilling note) marked it down as the closest relation here to the songs on 'This Year's Model', it fitted awkwardly into the scheme of things on an album whose sugar-sweetness threatened to decay – if not draw – Costello's lyrical teeth.

There *were* some memorable musical moments on 'Armed Forces', though, even if one or two of them did leave the listener wondering where they'd heard the melody before. 'Busy Bodies', for example, was an interesting attempt to dress up one of Costello's slighter lyrics on fashionable fornication in the album's second Abba-esque arrangement: 'Name Of The Game' was, appropriately, the song brought to mind this time. And if most reviewers picked up on the love song to a 'Party Girl' as having possible parallels with the recent object of Elvis' wayward affections, at least one lyrical couplet ('starts like fascination/ends up like a trance') dated from as long ago as 1976 and 'Jump Up' from D.P. Costello's demo tape. If Elvis was laughing to himself as he recycled his past, the glorious fade to 'Party Girl' with its 'Abbey Road' overtones would bring a smile to any Beatle fan's face.

Full marks to Costello, Lowe and The Attractions, then, for resisting the temptation to remodel last year's long player; but there remained the suspicion that under the shiny studio arrangements and all-pervasive double-tracked harmonies the 12 songs on view were rather less substantial than one had come to expect. And though The Attractions' playing fully justified their first co-billing on the record sleeve – a complex, double-sided foldover affair on the original UK issue, the inside's drip graphics sufficing on a conventional sleeve for the States – quality songs had, after all, been the foundation of Costello's success so far.

As if to illustrate that music criticism and popular acclaim have precious little in common, record buyers on both sides of the Atlantic fell upon 'Armed Forces' with undisguised delight. If Costello's new-wave leanings and aggression had hitherto alienated more mature audiences, then 'Armed Forces' disarmed his detractors with a grin. And as for the States, where anything remotely 'punk' had been treated with the utmost disdain, the time was right for Elvis to cash in on his new pop personality status. Nick Lowe: "A lot of Americans found (punk) hard to identify with… I think with myself or Elvis or Parker or Dury the approach is a lot easier for Americans to understand. There's almost an over-reaction – they like us too much, because they've been dying to get cracking but can't relate to The Damned." 'Armed Forces' swift rise through *Billboard's* Hot Hundred would soon prove the professor of pop's theory to be 101 per cent correct.

For Jake Riviera, the success of 'Armed Forces' in the States was clearly a great relief. Like Columbia label-mate Bruce Springsteen, Elvis made the break to a mass audience with his third album, just before the record label could attempt to write him off as a spent force. From 'Born To Run' onwards Springsteen was given the best of everything in terms of promotion and publicity: if success bred success, this was the first step on the stairway to stardom. Yet as events were to prove it would be all too easy to slip, leaving Costello's parting shot on 'Two Little Hitlers' – 'I will return, I will not burn' – sounding less like a promise than a despairing exclamation.

As was to become something of a tradition for Costello's albums, 'Armed Forces' was recorded in a remarkably short space of time – a mere two weeks at Eden Studios. The achievement is even more noteworthy when it's considered that five extra songs were declared surplus to requirements, making a total of 17 songs in all. Three have already been mentioned. Brinsley Schwarz's repertoire yielded 'Peace Love And Understanding', and this was released in three forms – as an album track on the US pressing of 'Armed Forces', replacing 'Sunday's Best', coupled with a wonderful version of Rodgers and Hart's 'My Funny Valentine' as that country's alternative to 'Oliver's Army' and in the UK as the B-side to Nick Lowe's 'American Squirm' single released in October 1978. Never one of Lowe's most noteworthy compositions 'American Squirm' failed to chart, but it has since become a collectors' item due to the B-side, credited to Nick Lowe and His Sound. Significantly, Nick wielded Elvis' personalised Jazzmaster guitar on the front sleeve, while its owner can dimly be seen peering through the window on the rear – if you're looking for him, that is.

The Dominion freebie, 'Talking In The Dark'/'Wednesday Week', has already been mentioned in passing; neither amounted to much more than out-takes. One of the final two tracks of the 'Armed Forces' sessions, the excellent mid-paced 'Tiny Steps', preceded the album's release as the B-side of 'Radio Radio', leaving 'Clean Money' as the sole song not yet accounted for. A rumbustious uptempo rocker, with Dave Edmunds joining The Attractions on backing vocals, it was not to surface publicly until late 1980. Meanwhile, though, its insistent playout chorus 'She won't take my love for tender/for tender' was recycled to become the main theme of a song of the same name on Elvis' next album. But let's not get *too* far ahead of ourselves here…

As the UK tour wound down, Costello took another turn in the confessional with Father Nicky Horne at Capital Radio. His selection veered widely between pop and parody, from The Left Banke's original of 'Walk Away Renee' to The Bay City Rollers' 'Rock And Roll Love Letter' via The Jackson Five and The Jam. An interesting pairing was Sandie Shaw's 'Girl Don't Come' and the debut single from a London band that updated the Shaw sound to perfection. The Pretenders recorded Nick Lowe's production of 'Stop Your Sobbing' at Eden Studios while The Attractions took a day off, Elvis footing the bill himself. Though the band went on to record their first album with Chris Thomas and not Lowe, it was a leg-up for which they were more than grateful.

Still in Capital's Euston Towers, Costello denounced the Dominion gigs as a mistake. He'd tried something different because he considered the Hammersmith Odeon and Rainbow Theatre "boring", but the Dominion had been "too plush". Suiting actions to words, he played the barn-like Hammersmith Palais, scene of many performances by his father, in February; but, as ever, there was to be no respite. The spadework in the States was finally paying off, and 'Armed Forces' entered the chart at number 46. The battle-weary Attractions packed their cases and headed West, little knowing how crucial this particular trip was to be.

Meanwhile, back at the Marquee Club in Wardour Street, something was stirring. Joe Jackson's sardonic delivery, his ear for a concise pop melody and willingness to jump on the Police-led bandwagon of post-punk pop with pace and panache, was possibly the biggest threat yet to Costello's home market. Sure, Graham Parker had been there first, but a lacklustre live album and his inability to penetrate the singles market kept him out of the picture. Jackson's mind was working along the lines of 'Oliver's Army', yet without the subversive slant. 'Is She Really Going Out With Him', the single that was to hit number 13 that summer, proffered alienation in an easily palatable form. 'Accidents Will Happen', an altogether more substantial song, made number 28, as Elvis unpacked his suitcase in yet another anonymous Holiday Inn on the verge of commercial success in the States.

The stakes were high, the strain well-nigh intolerable. Something had to give, and the first thing as it turned out was Costello's health. He contracted a stomach bug in Dallas – the city's revenge for his 'Less Than Zero' rewrite? – that caused the cancellation of a week's worth of shows. Live appearances were what the tour was all about, and with Elvis' attitude towards the press in mind Columbia arranged for local radio stations to act as unofficial sponsors for the date in their locality, hoping in this way to attract free publicity and maybe a live broadcast of the concert once tickets had sold out. A week's cancelled dates, then, put the whole campaign up against the clock – and cranked the pressure up still higher.

Given The Attractions' recent touring schedule, a break might well have been a wise decision. As it was, Costello and crew faced an unending series of soundchecks, coach-rides and publicity with rather less enthusiasm than is advisable for an act hoping to win friends and influence people. It was in the Holiday Inn at Columbus, Ohio, that three tours crossed and Elvis, Stephen Stills and Bonnie Bramlett found themselves sharing small talk at the bar. With hindsight, perhaps, it was inevitable that a veteran white soul singer (Bramlett), a refugee from Woodstock (Stills) and an emissary of the English new wave would have their differences of opinion, but no-one was prepared for what happened next.

According to reliable sources, some – if not all – parties concerned were the worse for drink. Costello's alleged dismissal of Ray Charles as an "ignorant blind nigger" and James Brown with similar contempt was followed by a free-for-all in which Elvis apparently bit the dust, "shaken but not stirred" as one report had it. Given the racism that exists to this day in the very fabric of the US popular music system, it was ironic that untypical remarks made in the heat of a drunken argument between parties clearly bent on outrage should have led to such a furore. Yet Costello had been foolish enough to allow the media he had spurned so often and so arrogantly the chance to wreak its revenge and undo countless months of touring in a matter of days.

Not that the tour thus far had been without incident. In St. Louis, Missouri, where a concert was sponsored for publicity purposes by radio station KSHE, Costello learned that a rival station had been playing 'Armed Forces' for somewhat longer than these Johnny-come-latelys. His response was to dedicate songs to the rival operation, reserving 'Radio Radio' for "all the local bastard radio stations that don't play our songs – and to KSHE". At a higher level, there was a suspicion that Columbia, Costello's US label, was not putting all the power it might have into promoting the artist – especially when the label refused Jake Riviera the funding to hire Shea Stadium after a competition for tickets to a free New York concert-hall gig brought some 25,000 applications. He responded by sending a vanload of shovels to the Columbia executives, an accompanying note remarking, "If you *really* want to bury my act I thought you could do with some help."

But Riviera's act, it seemed, was doing the job well enough already. 'Armed Forces' jumped to number 10 in the *Billboard* album charts by March 17, ironically the day after the bar-room brawl. It fell out of the Top Thirty by the third week of April – and, symbolically, it was replaced by the debut album from The Police, one of the few new acts to have matched Costello's gruelling tour schedules in previous months and a band who were unlikely to risk all that hard work for the sake of winning an argument. Police

protection was what Costello needed now – by the time he'd
reached New York in early April some 150 death threats had been
made against him. Suddenly the 'Dallas version' of 'Less Than Zero'
had lost its appeal.

Not since John Lennon rashly compared The Beatles' popularity to Jesus Christ had the American media pilloried a rock star so
relentessly. After a few drinks too many, the 'devil's advocate' who
provoked so many all-night discussions in the Flip City homestead
decided to see how far he could take things. As Costello revealingly
put it later, "I'm sure everybody's had occasion to go to absolute
extremes – even to say things you don't believe. Ask Lenny
Bruce." When someone asked Ray Charles what *he* thought, his
answer was tolerance itself. "Anyone could get drunk at least once
in his life," he said, adding: "Drunken talk isn't meant to be printed
in the paper, and people should judge Mr. Costello by his songs
rather than his stupid bar talk." That said, the remarks attributed to
Costello were disgraceful and should not be taken lightly. But as he
was about to find out, hell hath no fury like the media spurned...

In many ways, the tour never really gained the momentum
so desperately needed to push 'Armed Forces' to the top of the tree
and establish Costello as a major talent in the land of opportunity.
With 53 concerts in 69 days, one could understand if not sympathise
with the short sets that caused protests among audiences at Seattle
and Berkeley, California: at the former venue, the sound engineer
cleared the hall with high-pitched 'white' noise through the PA
system, while other members of the entourage dressed in army-
surplus fatigues to suit the tenor of the album/tour were apt to
pounce on (and mete out summary justice to) would-be bootleggers, photographers and stage invaders at the slightest provoca-
tion. If Costello was riding for a fall, it was time to clear the air –
something which a New York press conference on the 14th floor of
the Columbia building called at two hours' notice signally failed to
do.

The 50 or so newsmen assembled heard something
apparently less than an apology: "It was necessary for me to
outrage these people with the most obnoxious and offensive words
I could muster to bring the argument to a swift conclusion and rid
myself of their presence," he said. "It worked pretty good; it
started a fight." It was to prove something of a struggle, too, to
finish his two outstanding weeks of dates: the Capitol Theatre in
New Jersey, the New York Palladium, a string of New England
engagements and, firstly, an April Fools' Day series of clubland gigs
in downtown New York City at 6 pm, 9 pm and midnight. Finding
the clubs picketed by Rock Against Racism activists, Costello
responded by opening his set with 'I Stand Accused', then 'Accidents Will Happen'.

Back home, the incident was viewed in a somewhat different light; Costello's appearance at Rock Against Racism's Brockwell Park gig the previous September was still fresh in his fans' minds, while the national newspapers somehow failed to pick up on it. Ross McManus went into print as being "upset about these allegations against Elvis because I know they're not true... The race issue was always very important in our house. Elvis is no racist", and honour, on this side of the Atlantic at least, was satisfied. As for the States, though, it was to be 18 months before Costello ventured there again.

At home, Elvis' private life continued to fascinate the media rather more than his fights with fading rock stars. Although he continued to treat such intrusions with a suitably stony silence, a press report of Dave Edmunds' wedding reception in May 1979 (where Jake Riviera was best man) confirmed that the liaison of some nine months had ended, and that Elvis and wife Mary were back together again. An appearance in rather less select company – the Hammersmith Odeon audience attracted by The J. Geils Band – found him in the best of spirits, signing autographs and shaking hands. The couple's recent trip to Paris might well have been a second honeymoon – even though, as Costello confessed to a wellwisher, they'd seen The J. Geils band twice there too.

But while the weather forecast for Elvis' personal life read fine, calm and sunny, storm clouds loomed for Radar Records. Their artist roster remained small and, while Costello and Nick Lowe continued to sell albums in reasonable quantities and hit the bottom regions of the singles Top Forty, there seemed a remarkable lack of adventure from Jake Riviera, the man who set trends with Stiff that were the envy of every multi-million major label in the country. These were undoubtedly what WEA thought they were buying when they agreed to fund Radar; their decision to wind the label up would, perhaps, net them Costello and Lowe without the overheads of funding a separate label. But Warner and his Brothers were mixing it with Jake Riviera; would force of numbers (of dollars) prevail, or would the little man win through? The world awaited developments.

Soul Attractions

Tucked in behind the entrance to Camden Town underground station, Rock On is the kind of record shop most busy commuters would give something less than a second glance. Yet to those in the know, Rock On is a veritable goldmine, a treasure trove of old, rare and sought-after sounds – country soul, blues and rockabilly – for the cognoscenti. Yet bargains don't come cheap; the proprietors, who started with a stall in Soho Market immortalised by Phil Lynott in Thin Lizzy's 'The Rocker', value their vinyl realistically. So it was a sure bet that when Elvis Costello emerged from the establishment in October 1979 clutching an armful of singles and albums, he'd invested a fair proportion of his allowance – £50 is the figure that has passed into pop legend. But would it be money well spent?

Costello spent his summer closeted in the studio, postponing any decisions on his own career by immersing himself in the affairs of others – his cure for the bar room blues was to produce the debut album for The Specials. The multi-racial seven-piece band from Coventry was acclaimed as the 'next big thing' by both a rock press waiting for another 'new wave' and an audience who watched as the spontaneity of punk disappeared down the ever-open mouth of the music machine while the musicians who supplied the vital, raw sounds of 1977 became the self-satisfied pop stars of 1979.

The Specials' first, independently released single, 'Gangsters', shot up the national charts on the basis of their live act – steaming helpings of ska and bluebeat, served up with humour, energy and a fair amount of aggression. The single won them a lucrative contract with Chrysalis, who beat several majors to their signature by offering them a custom label, 2-Tone. Yet faced with the problem of recording their first long-player for such high stakes, they needed someone to help them channel their raw, undisciplined energy on to vinyl.

It would have been quite a challenge for an experienced producer; a newcomer to the job like Elvis could well have found he'd bitten off more than he could chew. But three years with Nick

Lowe had obviously taught him *something*: dispensing with any idea of making the album sound deliberately dated in Sixties ska style, he gave it a plain, no nonsense production of which 'Basher' would have been justly proud. The major task with a band like The Specials was to arrange each song into some kind of cohesive pattern, especially since a two-man horn section was used to beef up some of the numbers. Given that many of The Specials saw the inside of a recording studio for the first time when they recorded their debut single, the results achieved were clearly a credit both to them and their producer.

A skanking cover of 'A Message To You Rudy' was to bring them more singles success when culled from the album in October, but it was only one of several strong tracks that made the album perhaps the year's most memorable. Costello would also remember the summer of 1979 for his second Top Five hit – an eventuality even his staunchest fans couldn't have expected with no new material scheduled until the year's end. While he'd been busy producing, his own producer had been doing a spot of moonlighting...

Nick Lowe kept his parallel career going the other side of the mixing desk by renewing his on-off association with Dave Edmunds. The end result of this, the first all-Rockpile project ('Get It' having consisted of several sessions stitched together) was 'Tracks On Wax', released in 1978 and bolstered by some happier live dates than previously. In short, both parties felt the association worth compromising for – something Costello would never have contemplated.

Lowe, always a prolific writer, hogged the lion's share of this album's composer credits, since Edmunds was notably shy about recording his own material. So it was that, when gathering songs for his next album, the soft-spoken Welshman plucked up the courage to approach Costello. "He was in a studio at the time," he smilingly remembered, "and he whacked out 'Girls Talk' at a million miles an hour. It was a good song but it wasn't anything like the way it turned out..." The track Elvis gave him was first aired on 'Repeat When Necessary', Edmunds' fifth solo LP released in June 1979 – and while the album only scraped into the Top Forty, 'Girls Talk' proved a far better commercial proposition as a single. Combined, by strange coincidence, with Edmunds' version of Huey Lewis' 'Bad Is Bad', it swiftly climbed the Top Twenty in July to peak at number 4.

It was a catchy song with rather more substance than much of Edmunds' usual fare, but with a commercial gloss its composer would have been unlikely to give it. Riding on a wave of multi-tracked acoustic guitars and Everly Brothers vocals knocked out in characteristic fashion by Edmunds and Lowe, the words were the last thing to reach the listeners' consciousness – yet when the bare bones of Costello's one minute 56 second demo reached a wider audience on a B-side some months later it was evident how much attention was lavished on the song to turn it into three and a half minutes of superior chart single. Yet Costello has always regarded the song as his own, and, when he began his 1984 solo concerts with it, the audience response reciprocated that feeling. A tale of snatched snippets and half-overheard whispers, it might or might not, as the *NME's* Max Bell suggested, have been "one on the nose for Bebe Buell", but its typically sharp wordplay and confidential delivery made Costello's version almost a different song entirely. As Dave Edmunds commented, "There are lots of different ways of doing it. I heard a supermarket version of 'Girls Talk' that was absolutely hilarious."

Costello's final act before shutting himself in with The Specials was to play an unscheduled set at a Radar Records party in his hometown of Liverpool, where he'd been "visiting Mum". An estimated 400 people crowded aboard the Mersey Ferry *Royal Iris* to see The Yachts and Clive Langer was surprised and delighted to find Elvis and The Attractions opening proceedings at a clip. "Hi there," chirped an unusually affable Costello. "We're a little nervous 'cos we haven't played for a while, but we thought we'd come and surprise you." But was his choice of the Merseybeats' 'I Stand Accused' as opener a wry reflection of past troubles or a pointer to his new direction on record? Back in Elvis' youth, the Cunard ocean liners plied their trade from Liverpool to the Americas at a time when air travel was beyond the reach of the working man. With the advent of the Jumbo Jet Cunard sold off most of their fleet, upped anchor and relocated to Southampton, yet it was an Atlantic crossing that Costello had in mind to rejuvenate his music. And though the *Royal Iris* wouldn't get him there, his trip to Rock On provided him with the inspiration he needed.

Perhaps the easiest course of action in an attempt to find a new sound perspective would have been to find another producer: "A change is as good as a rest," Nick Lowe hinted to the press as far back as May. And having produced a Top Five album in The Specials' debut, many artists would have wondered if they needed a producer anyway. Yet Nick's contribution was to be more than just the silly liner notes to the finished article which, like the deliberately dated geometrical cover design with its 'pre-worn' look, tried rather too hard to be Sixties. After all, the Brinsleys had always had a sneaking fondness for soul, notably Allen Tousaint's 'Wonder Woman' recorded on the 'Greasy Truckers Party' live LP and their (unreleased) version of William Bell and Judy Clay's 'Private Number'.

The team of Nick Lowe and engineer Roger Bechirian may have been retained but the action shifted from Acton's Eden Studios to Wisseloord in The Netherlands. And any suspicion that Elvis might have forgotten to pack his stack of soul singles was dispelled by the opening track. 'I Can't Stand Up For Falling Down', a mouthful of a title that ranked with Costello's wordiest, was unearthed from the B-side of Sam and Dave's 'Smooth Talk' single, vintage 1967. Together with the previously mentioned 'I Stand Accused' from the Merseybeat archives, it stood alongside no less than 18 new Costello compositions. Ten tracks a side – now *there* was a flashback to the young Declan's dog-eared 'Motown Chartbusters' he'd carried under his arm to every teenage party he attended. Yet with a total running time of some 47 minutes, it was plain that this score of songs was unlikely to outstay its welcome. And though only a couple broke the two-and-a-half minute barrier, there were enough ideas, hooks, puns and styles to both delight and confuse the listener.

Bearing in mind that 'Armed Forces' delivered the mass pop audience to Elvis on a plate, this seemed a wilful attempt to change not only musical tack but offer his listeners more material than could possibly be digested in a single sitting. Several of these songs – 'High Fidelity', 'B Movie' and 'Opportunity' among them – had been woodshedded in live performance long before the band entered the studio, predating even Elvis' shopping expedition. Yet, as Costello himself later commented, they "sounded like clichéd new wave music… (the album) would have come out sounding something like a cross between 'Armed Forces' and 'This Year's Model'."

The remodelling of 'B Movie' was particularly apparent: once an uptempo rocker, it metamorphosed on album into a jazzy nightclub ballad, while 'I Can't Stand Up' went the other way, a slowish number now taken at breakneck pace. Lyrics ('New Amsterdam') and/or titles ('Possession', previously known as 'Idle Hands') were changed, too, indicating Costello's determination that this album would indeed be very different to any or all of its predecessors. Eight of the songs to appear on the album were demoed before departure at the tiny 8-track Archipelago Studios in London's Pimlico: the only one of these tentative song-sketches to surface legally was the first take of 'Black And White World' which appeared on the 'Taking Liberties'/'Ten Bloody Marys' compilation in 1980.

'Get Happy..' was, needless to say, an ironic title. The best soul music has always celebrated pain and gloried in grief. It might have been schlock-pop tunesmith Neil Diamond who said that when you take the blues and make a song, you sing them out again – but then again, this collection of celebratory soul anthems kicked

'Armed Forces' plumb into the middle of the road. If he couldn't bring himself to be happy, Elvis could still sing out his blues in song – and there were more than a few diamonds here. The album's two cover versions provided the model for *this* year's mood: with 'I Can't Stand Up For Falling Down', a double-tracked Elvis (playing Sam *and* Dave) had every intention of fighting on even though heartbreak had knocked him clean off his feet, while 'I Stand Accused' provided the Merseybeats' variation on the theme of Luther Ingram's 'If Loving You Is Wrong (I Don't Want To Be Right)'. The raw blast of Bruce Thomas' harmonica underlined the facts – and *nothing* could stop this man from spelling it out.

The first person singular in both titles was no coincidence: the style Elvis selected meant that this *had* to be a more personal album than its predecessor. It was more positive, too: instead of the "utter, complete loser" we'd heard on 'My Aim Is True' this was the work of a man whose determination grew with every rebuff – 'Climb Every Mountain' wasn't in it…

Borrowed licks and familiar vocal inflections abounded, giving ready ammunition to critics – yet where the 'Armed Forces' steals had been sly undercover affairs, this was a record that was openly proud of its heritage. "Each song I could go through and tell you which band we were being: Al Green on one, The Four Tops on another" confessed the perpetrator of these misdeeds. Yet The Four Tops' Levi Stubbs would have been proud to lend his name to 'High Fidelity', a stomping pianoforte romp through Motown, while Steve Cropper's celebrated two-string guitar riff had rarely been heard to better advantage than on 'Temptation', a closer-than-close relation to the MGs' 'Time is Tight'. Even when the actual songs themselves consisted of little more than the germ of an idea, as in 'Love For Tender', sheer exuberance brought The Attractions through unscathed.

Apart from the two covers that made it on to the finished album, a couple more of Elvis' 'Rock On' purchases made it to Holland in his flight bag. And though The Attractions' stab at the Contours' Smokey Robinson-penned 'First I Look At The Purse' was not to be released, the northern soul of Van McCoy's 'Getting Mighty Crowded' (Elvis would have bought Betty Everett's 1964 version on Vee-Jay) was later to be aired as an American single as well as a British B-side. Unlike Larry Williams' 'Slow Down', the only other track from the Dutch sessions to remain in the vaults, it hadn't yet shown up in The Attractions' stage set – in fact it would be 1984 before it was dusted down and given a live airing. A nod to his more recent past came from 'Human Touch', whose ska sound-alike tribute to The Specials not only superseded the instrumental version of 'Gangsters' that had cropped up in some late-1979 concerts but showed yet another musical facet of The Attractions.

With so many sets of song words to come up with, Costello plundered his past: 'King Horse', in many ways an obvious (but overlooked) follow-up to 'Oliver's Army' with similar pounding piano and singalong chorus, used lyrics from "a song I wrote in 1976 – I can't remember the title", while 'New Amsterdam' harked back to his youth, 'the old days of Liverpool and Rotherhithe' and how in London he'd still felt 'like an exile'; though born in the capital, he always considered himself a Merseysider. Suitably, given the intensely personal nature of that lyric, he played all the instruments on the track himself, producing what was almost a modern folk song in waltz time and a refreshing contrast in style to the rest of the album.

Lyrically, then, it came as some relief to find that Costello had recharged his batteries – yet the past year's slump in form wasn't totally inexplicable. Most songwriters find their second album suffers in comparison with their debut, largely because with the best of their old songs gone and a touring schedule to meet they find it hard to produce the goods on time. Costello postponed this creative trough by writing two 'first albums' – one recorded solo, the other with a band – and coming off the road in late 1979 in the aftermath of Columbus helped him overcome the comparative lack of inspiration in the 'Armed Forces' material. The wordplay, as ever, was there – "you lack lust/you're so lacklustre" he punningly complained in 'Possession' – but the irony and anger of old were once more present along with the wit. And with 20 songs his imagination had ample opportunity to run riot.

Appropriately, then, 'Riot Act' closed the album with a measured, aching vocal performance that surely ranked as his best ever. But the disquieting message between the vocal lines suggested that Costello was more bruised by the past year than anyone believed. "Trying to be bad is bad enough," he complains, later adding "But it doesn't look like I'm gonna be around much anymore." Had Elvis Costello finally tired of his public image? And what effect would this have on his music? While the answers remained unknown, his fans should have seen enough by now to expect the unexpected.

For now, though, expectation remained the name of the game as Jake Riviera's legal tussle with WEA continued to block the album's public release. In a friendly gesture of support, The Specials offered Costello the use of their 2-Tone label through which to release a single. The plan nearly worked, too; 13,000 copies of 'I Can't Stand Up For Falling Down' bore the famous 2-Tone gangster logo, yet were never distributed to the shops because legal papers started to fly. Although the situation remained unclear at the beginning of 1980, Capital Radio was happily playing an acetate copy of the single, even though Warners allegedly took out a court injunction to stop the BBC doing likewise. Meanwhile, the album was a matter of three months old, with little immediate chance of reaching the public via radio or record shop.

Suddenly, though, things started to move like an earlier-than-usual spring thaw. A month-long tour was announced, exclusively taking in towns never visited before. All the dates were pre-advertised in local papers to ensure fair play, all venues were unseated and tickets pegged at a uniform £3. With the tour due to start at West Runton Pavilion, East Anglia, on 1 March it was evident that the vinyl pipeline would soon be unblocked too; the last thing Jake Riviera would be likely to do would be to send Elvis on tour with nothing to promote.

Sure enough, by the beginning of February the last pieces of the jigsaw slipped into place. F-Beat Records, as the new company was to be known, would "be doing all marketing, promotion and advertising, and WEA will press and distribute the records. The deal is completely separate from the previous Radar agreement." A good old-fashioned British compromise saw Riviera 'free' again, though still in close proximity to the corporate clutches of Warner Brothers. And, as always in such matters, the only winners were the legal fraternity: "I've been cited so many times I'm beginning to think I'm a UFO," quipped a rueful Andrew Lauder. Costello celebrated the deal with a spot of public rehearsal, guesting unannounced at the Liverpool and Bradford dates of the Rockpile/Fabulous Thunderbirds tour as the unlikely-named Horace Barlow Experience. In echoes of Stiff's enthusiastic marketing campaign for 'My Aim Is True', double-page ads for the new album appeared in the music press, announcing that 'Get Happy..' would be a "record to stand you on your feet." If Jake Riviera had still to prove that F-Beat could do likewise, at the very least he'd bought himself a pair of better-fitting shoes to ease the pain.

The tape that D.P. Costello, solo singer, sent to Charlie Gillett's radio show in 1976 made a surprise re-appearance in late 1979 when it was advertised in *New Musical Express* as a prize in a special Christmas competition. "This has to be the ultimate collectors' item," boasted the not so small print – but in the event the tape stayed out of the Costello collectors' clutches. Two weeks later the prize had metamorphosed into "Two days in the studio with Nick Lowe", after much behind-the-scenes activity ensured that Elvis' back pages would be turned only at the behest of their author – though the message didn't get through to the bootlegging fraternity.

There *was*, however, a welcome spinoff for those who entered the tape competition and whose musical talents might not have met Mr. Lowe's high standards. Certain lucky entrants who answered the questions correctly found themselves in receipt of a belated Christmas present in the form of a copy of 'Talking In The Dark'/'Wednesday Week' left over from the 1978 Dominion dates and a couple of tickets to a secret gig at Hammersmith's Clarendon Hotel on 18 January 1980. The gig was one of many Attractions shows to be taped – a bootleg entitled 'Clarendon' duly appeared – and led to speculation as to whether an official live album would be released.

As it transpired, though, this was far from the only Attractions concert to be preserved on tape. In 1983 Costello was to reveal that at least one gig of every tour had been recorded, so any collection for commercial release "would have to be…one of those documentary live albums rather than any specific gig," stressing that "I've usually got so many songs that I'm keen to put out my new material." Such reticence has led to Elvis becoming one of the most bootlegged artists ever, a distinction he shares with Bruce Springsteen, another much-admired singer and songwriter who has never chosen to release an official live album. Elvis' attitude, not surprisingly, is one of disapproval "not because I don't get royalties for it but I can judge for myself what is suitable for a larger audience." One track that *did* pass his acid test was a live version of 'The Imposter', recorded at Hammersmith at the Concerts for Kampuchea the previous December and released on the double album of that event in March.

Costello-watchers were surprised to see Elvis make a rare television appearance in February. The programme was 'Tiswas', a children's free-for-all in which the highlight was the imprisonment (and dousing of the audience) in a contraption known as 'The Cage'. Although no-one was quite forward enough to volunteer Elvis as a captive, he even swung the odd bucket in fun and appeared relatively at ease. Yet as if to underline the fact that Riviera and crew were back in business, press and photographers were banned from the first night of the tour. That couldn't have pleased Clive Langer, who'd willingly accepted the invitation of his support act on the Mersey cruise to step aboard in a similar position; but this tour was to prove the first step in a profitable songwriting and production partnership between the two singers. And though Clive was eventually to become Elvis' producer, their first collaboration saw the roles reversed as Costello produced two tracks on Langer's 'Splash' album, released later that year.

It was now well over a year since Elvis' last vinyl venture, even longer since his last major UK shows. It was time to make a reappearance, since it was now a favoured pastime of the media to put forward 'Costello clones' as substitutes for the real thing. You didn't have to be Joe Jackson to qualify, either: Roogalator's Danny Adler (dark-rimmed glasses, Jazzmaster guitar, one-time Stiff re-

cording artist) was one of the first in the frame, while an unknown
Irish folk-singer named Clive Culbertson was bylined, "He's never
worn glasses, he's two stone overweight and he's never hit a
woman in his life" by a music paper that should remain nameless –
yes, it was *that* silly.

Moon Martin, like Adler a genuine talent the press found
difficult to define, was labelled – literally – by his own record
company via an 'Elvis soundalike' sticker on his 'Escape From
Domination' album, while the Original Mirrors' debut LP wore a
suspiciously Costello-esque graphic design on its sleeve. The madness went on: *Melody Maker's* Allan Jones went overboard about
Any Trouble, a four-piece swiftly signed up (ironically by Stiff)
whose singer, Clive Gregson, had an (un)fortunately Elvisian set of
tubes: the backlash from the remainder of the media almost crip-
pled the band, who survived only two albums with Stiff before the
label answered their question in the affirmative. And then there
was The Jags, a London four-piece whose 'Back Of My Hand' hit
was a perfect Costello pastiche. It worked once, but with the return
of the real thing they vanished. In view of recent events, Elvis
spared 'em the court case…

The formation of F-Beat more or less coincided with Jake
Riviera finally managing to untangle the knotty contractual problems that prevented Rockpile, his other major interest, from recording under their own name as a band. Yet curiously their first
and only 'group' release, 1980's 'Seconds Of Pleasure', was far less
cohesive and unified than any of their leaders' solo projects. "I was
expecting something to happen that would be more than the sum of
the parts," commented Edmunds later. "I didn't want it to sound
like a few tracks off a Dave Edmunds album and a few tracks off a
Nick Lowe album, but that's exactly what it was."

It wasn't long before Rockpile, never less than a knockout
live band whatever the temperature of their current output on wax,
split up. A series of disagreements apparently came to a head when
Riviera proffered a set of papers for Edmunds' signature. "And if I
had (signed) that would've been it. No control any more of anything. Not with the record company we went with, what singles
were released, what the covers or the artwork would be like…the
next thing I knew, the band had broken up." It was just one man's
side of the story, and certainly Nick Lowe had no qualms about
remaining with F-Beat and their genial supremo, but Edmunds'
hightailing to Arista made the casual observer wonder what else
was going on in the wings.

For Elvis Costello, early 1980 and the 'Get Happy..' project
had been relatively successful. 'High Fidelity', the second single
(and his first to appear in 12-inch form) reached number 30 in April,
while a whole EP was constructed around 'New Amsterdam',

released in June with three Costello-produced efforts augmenting his album track. That reached number 36 in Britain. In the States, though, he was still chasing his first hit single, and it must have been galling to see Nick Lowe reaping the benefits of their corporate touring with the Top Twenty-riding 'Cruel To Be Kind' while his own fortunes slid in the aftermath of the Stills/Bramlett incident. The album-buying public seemed more prepared to forgive and forget, though, and 'Get Happy..', aided by airplay on soul radio stations, made it to number 11 despite his year-round absence from their shores.

Though Elvis was keeping a low profile in the States for the time being, his songs were still being promoted there – by an unlikely source. Linda Ronstadt, the West Coast-based singer whose former backing band had become The Eagles and who was to achieve similar success as an interpreter of other people's songs, had taken her first leaf out of the Costello songbook by including a version of 'Alison' on her 'Living In The USA' album in late 1978. Quite apart from the song's obvious unsuitability for a female singer, its personal significance to Elvis couldn't have improved matters. February 1980, though, saw triple trouble when her 'Mad Love' LP was found to contain no less than three Costello compositions – 'Party Girl', 'Talking In The Dark' and 'Girls Talk'.

Though Ronstadt's 'Alison' passed without comment from the songwriter concerned, he happened to be a guest on Radio 1's 'Round Table' review programme when he heard 'Mad Love' for the first time. Predictably, Elvis offered some forthright opinions. "I never want to hear that sheer torture again." he rumbled. "She should stop making 'Top Of The Pops' records that sell at Woolworths. The backing tracks sound exactly like ours and the dreadful vocals…a waste of vinyl." The winsome Linda made this her 'new wave' LP, bowing to national pride by recording a clutch of songs from an obscure American 'punk' named Mark Goldenburg of the even more obscure Cretones. Yet the fact that 1984 saw her release an album of vintage standards in the company of Nelson Riddle and his strings suggested that she'd taken Elvis' strangled warning – "please, please, don't record *any* of my songs" – to heart.

Looked at dispassionately, it was an intriguingly paradoxical twelve months. On the face of it, the Columbus incident carelessly squandered one and a half years of hard work in trying to break the United States – yet Costello's next move, a celebration of American soul rivalled only by Bowie's 'Young Americans', was the best response possible to charges of musical bigotry. And though US sales of his previous album had fallen off sharply, 'Get Happy' was received enthusiastically – a fact that, together with Linda Ronstadt's well-meaning attempts to cover his songs, meant that despite his self-enforced absence more Americans were now buying or listening to Elvis Costello songs than ever before.

To take the Bowie analogy one step further, 'Young Americans' was a watershed album that marked the end of a less than fertile period for the enigmatic performer and, after a false start with 'Station To Station', led to the landmark 'Low' and 'Heroes' sets that would prove so influential to Eighties rock. Could Costello follow in Bowie's footsteps? Would this mark the beginning of a facinating new phase of his career or had it merely been a stylistic diversion of no real consequence? And with his career spectacularly re-launched in Britain on a new label, could a man whose creative process thrived on the darker side of emotional life cope with success? Only time would tell.

Above: Flip City, 1974. Left to right: Steve Hazelhurst (lead guitar), Declan McManus (rhythm guitar, vocals), Mich Kent (bass), Dickie Faulkener (percussion, vocals), Malcolm Dennis (drums) and manager Ken Smith.
(Pete Brown)

Left: Declan McManus marries Mary Burgoyne, 1974. Best man is Flip City bassist Mich Kent.
(Pete Brown)

Below: Flip City, 1975. Left to right, back row: Mich Kent, Declan McManus, Malcolm Dennis; front row: Steve Hazelhurst, Dickie Faulkener.
(Mich Kent)

Above: The 'Operations Room' at Stiff Records, Alexander Street, Bayswater, in late 1977. Left to right: graphic designer Barney Bubbles, Suzanne Spiro (who would later marry Bruce Thomas), Jake Riviera, Cynthia Lowell, general manager Paul Conroy and tour manager Des Brown. (Barry Plummer)

Right: Declan McManus, 1974. (Pete Brown)

Below: Elvis and The Attractions, outside the Stiff HQ in Alexander Street, Bayswater, in 1977. Left to right: Bruce Thomas, Pete Thomas, Elvis, Steve Nieve. (Barry Plummer)

Top left: Elvis performs at Dingwalls Dance Hall, Camden Lock, July 1977. Earlier the same day he'd been arrested for obstruction (busking) outside the Hilton Hotel where CBS Records executives gathered for a sales conference.
(Barry Plummer)

Above: Pumping It Up. Elvis performing on the opening night of the Stiff Records package tour at High Wycombe Town Hall, October 3, 1977.
(Barry Plummer)

Left: Jake Riviera, aka Andrew Jakeman, 1977.
(Barry Plummer)

Above: Elvis with personally customised Fender Jazzmaster at the Rock Against Racism concert, Brockwell Park, Brixton, 1978.
(Barry Plummer)

Right: Elvis performs to 15,000 disinterested Santana fans at the Crystal Palace Bowl, September 1977, a rare mistake during the hectic months of Elvis' spectacular rise to fame.
(Barry Plummer)

Above: Elvis, flanked by The Attractions, performs at the Rock Against Racism concert at Brockwell Park, Brixton, 1978. (Barry Plummer)

Left: Dave Edmunds and Nick Lowe on stage with Rockpile at the Concerts for Kampuchea, Hammersmith Odeon, Christmas 1979. (Barry Plummer)

Top right: Elvis and The Attractions, 1979. Left to right: Elvis, Pete Thomas, Steve Nieve, Bruce Thomas. (Chris Gabrin)

Right: Elvis on stage during the Concerts For Kampuchea, Hammersmith Odeon, London, Christmas 1979. Attractions bassist Bruce Thomas is on the right. (Barry Plummer)

Above: Elvis takes the stage at the Royal Albert Hall on January 7, 1982, with the Royal Philharmonic Orchestra temporarily depping for The Attractions, to perform material from 'Almost Blue'.
(Steve Rapport/LFI)

Left: Elvis at The Clarendon, Hammersmith, January 1980.
(G. Swaine)

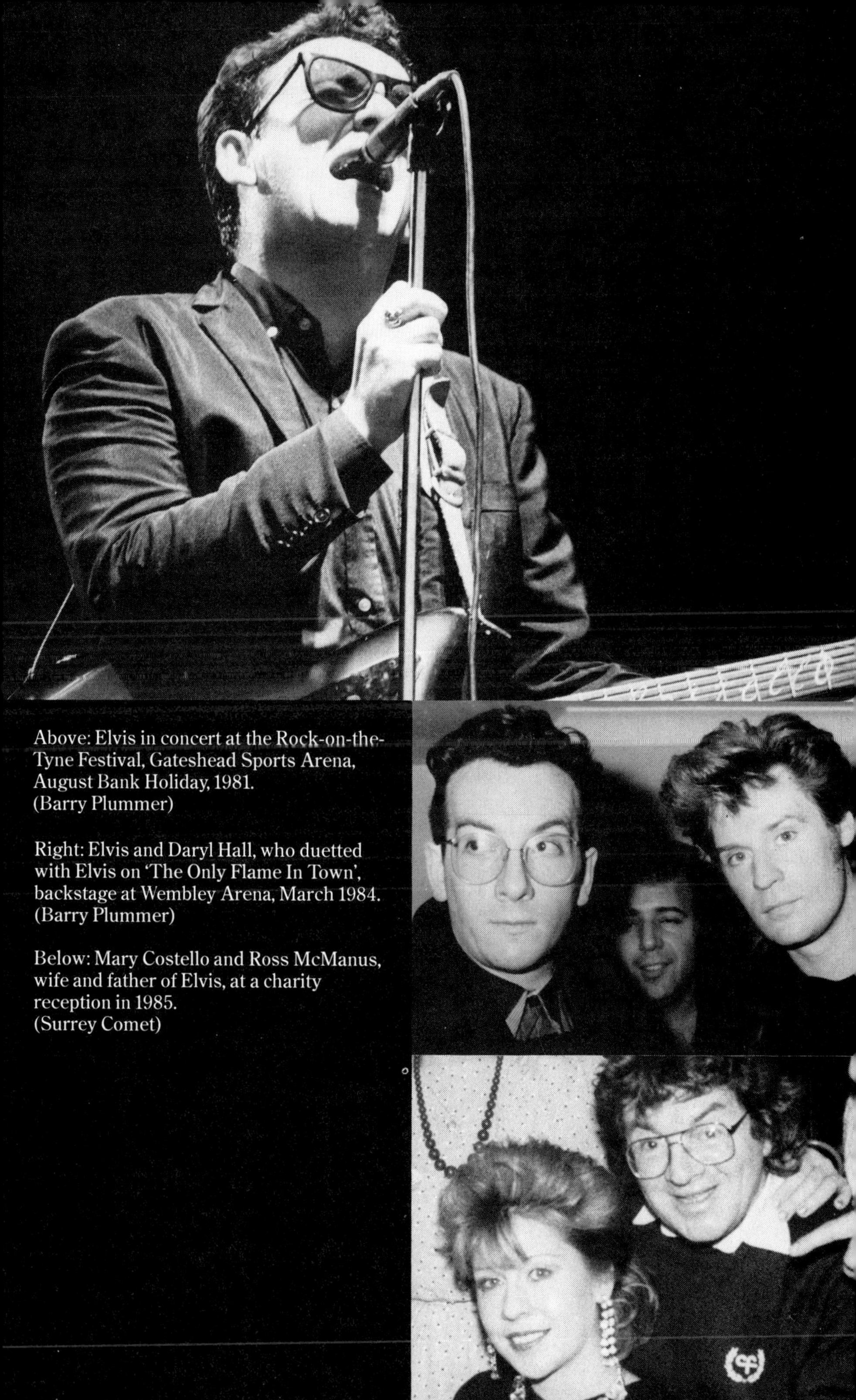

Above: Elvis in concert at the Rock-on-the-Tyne Festival, Gateshead Sports Arena, August Bank Holiday, 1981.
(Barry Plummer)

Right: Elvis and Daryl Hall, who duetted with Elvis on 'The Only Flame In Town', backstage at Wembley Arena, March 1984.
(Barry Plummer)

Below: Mary Costello and Ross McManus, wife and father of Elvis, at a charity reception in 1985.
(Surrey Comet)

An Album To Trust

If Elvis Costello had had his way, then 'Riot Act', the last of 'Get Happy..'s 20 tracks, would have been the final word his public would have heard from him. When he'd sung "It doesn't look like I'm going to be around much anymore", he really meant it. The madness of the past months was hitting him and he even admitted turning to drugs. "Any is too many," he explained when recalling the period in happier circumstances. The end of the 'Get Happy..' tour, though, saw him slump into a depression inspired by the knowledge that an audience that knew him only from television appearances was only interested in hits. "A lot of people came to hear 'Oliver's Army' and 'I Can't Stand Up'," he complained. "I just felt that I hadn't really got the bulk of songs over to a lot of people…I didn't want to be one of those one or two-number singers like Gene Pitney or somebody."

No, when recording 'Get Happy..' he'd intended it to be his last record. After the tour "I decided I didn't want to go on anymore and left the group. I just didn't see any point to it." On hearing the news, Steve Nieve's reaction was to jet off for an American holiday before the band's final commitment to a summer European tour for which they were still contracted. Accidents will happen, however, and when Steve was involved in a bad car crash while on vacation it's debatable who it shook up more – him or his boss several thousand miles away. "I realised I was being a bit spoilt," admitted Costello, who decided to fill the gap in the ranks in an unusual way by going to The Rumour for a temporary replacement. While the smart money would have been on keyboardist Bob Andrews as Nieve's deputy, Elvis chose lead guitarist Martin Belmont.

The tour was, understandably, a little more ragged than the well-rehearsed Attractions at full strength, but the challenge seemed to provide Costello with the motivation he needed. He turned to the organ on a couple of numbers, but mostly played rhythm to Belmont's spiky lead on such 'new' covers as Sonny Boy Williamson's 'Help Me' and Presley's 'Little Sister'. The visual implications of the line-up change were as interesting as the musical ones: lanky six-footer Belmont provided almost too much of a distraction alongside Elvis, occasionally threatening to invade his centre-stage position.

If the tour gave Costello a kick (in more ways than one), it was rewarding for Belmont too. "I just think I'm really lucky to have been asked to play with the most talented guys around," he said. As to whether he'd consider switching allegiance from Parker to Costello, he commented mysteriously, "I've actually been tempted, though I've not been asked." And though he never actually *was* asked to join The Attractions full-time, he played on the sessions for the next album, eventually ending up in the mid Eighties as a member of Nick Lowe's Cowboy Outfit. Yet his major contribution to the Elvis Costello story was in helping to re-kindle the singer's appetite for touring and recording.

The Attractions welcomed Steve back to the fold that August with two open-air appearances; one in Gateshead near Newcastle, the other rather further afield at Canada's Heatwave Festival, held at a speedway track 50 miles or so from Toronto. Extensive touring – or was it just Elvis' new-found zest for it? – wiped away the memory of their first open-air appearance back in 1977 at Crystal Palace, and their headliner over Rockpile, Talking Heads, The Pretenders and The Rumour (Martin Belmont again) ensured that the few North American fans they played to (this was their only 1980 date on that continent) went home happy.

The band's other engagement before heading to the studio to cut a new album was rather more low-key: in fact they were billed not as The Attractions but as Otis Westinghouse and The Lifts. The reason for such anonymity during their three-night 'residency' at the Albany Empire in Southeast London was so as not to take the publicity from headliners Squeeze, who were bidding farewell to keyboard player (and latterly TV personality) Jools Holland. Why should Costello and Co. be supporting Squeeze, you might ask? That was a question echoed by *NME's* Danny Baker: "If he was doing this for fun and a favour, you'd never have guessed-…no room for smiles, no breaks between songs, no musical gags, nothing was relaxed."

No, something was definitely afoot. And back in the dressing room, Squeeze guitarist Glenn Tilbrook realised it too. "On the final night they went on before us and Elvis played all his best-known numbers – one after the other." The reason for this 'battle of the bands' was to become clear when Jake Riviera made his move to manage Squeeze, one of Britain's most promising 'new-wave' combos; he obviously found they measured up favourably to the toughest of live opposition. Riviera clearly saw Squeeze as the ideal third force to complement The Attractions and Rockpile, while Elvis himself had a high opinion of the band's songwriters Chris Difford and Glenn Tilbrook – so high, in fact, that their 'Cool For Cats' and 'Argy Bargy' albums were required listening for The Attractions even before their commercial release.

The public party in Holland's honour concluded with both bands on stage together, a development that led Costello to rehearse the Stax classic 'Private Number' with Glenn Tilbrook as a duet. Also in The Attractions' set that week was Smokey Robinson's '(You Gotta Walk) Don't Look Back', a 1965 hit for The Temptations – but if Costello was looking forward with renewed enthusiasm, there was a temptation to forget that his determination to be his own man was no less great. Danny Baker's *New Musical Express* report of the after-gig festivities concluded with the fact that when Elvis was given a party hat he put it on "but as soon as the person who gave it to him went off (he) crumpled it up and threw it away."

With the recent breaks in The Attractions' punishing tour schedules, Steve, Bruce and Pete might have been excused for not knowing what to do with all this unaccustomed spare time. Both the Thomases were family men (Bruce having met and married Suzanne Spiro, Jake Riviera's former secretary, who'd taken his call for the audition in 1977) and had their home life to occupy them. It wasn't surprising, then, to find bachelor boy Steve becoming most active on the session front.

His first spell of moonlighting was with a little-known group called Twist, whose one and only album, 'This Is Your Life', appeared in 1979. The only semi-famous musicians in the band were Andy Pask (bass, later Landscape) and Jimmy Edwards (vocals, currently with Rick Buckler's Time UK) – yet, since Steve roped in his boss to help out with the backing vocals, the album has since acquired a certain value among Costello collectors. Rather more easily obtainable was his work with ex-Audience vocalist Howard Werth, whose half 'n' half album of R&B and originals, 'Six Of One', emerged on Demon in 1982; had Werth been alive and kicking in 1977, a man of his pedigree would surely have become a Stiff. Nieve was also to contribute to records by Carmel (her first single, 'Bad Day'), Nick Lowe, Bobby Henry, The Photos, Nick Heyward and Specials drummer John Bradbury's JB's Allstars.

Apart from pursuing solo session careers, there was another way the three Attractions could occupy themselves – record an album of their own. The seeds were sown by Elvis' decision to split; even now, it would be interesting to see what they could offer without him. Roger Bechirian was selected as producer – as Nick Lowe's engineer, he had much to prove in his new role as any of the others – and great things were expected of 'Mad About The Wrong Boy' on its release in September 1980. One of the reasons for such expectation was 'Single Girl', a taster for the album that appeared a couple of months in advance.

'Single Girl', a lyrically vacuous yet fairly catchy pop tune, was composed by the quaintly named songwriting partnership of Brain and Hart – yet their affiliation to Elvis' Plangent Visions music publishing company suggests the guilty parties to be Steve Nieve and his girlfriend Fay ('Farrah Fuckit Minor') Hart. B&H were also responsible for the title track and 'Sad About Girls', one of only two of the 16 sub three-minute songs (the other being the quirky 'Damage') to make the occasional appearance in the live set with Elvis; no solo promotional dates were ever played. The remainder of the album was more or less split between Steve Nieve, writing in his own name, and the rhythm section of Bruce and Pete Thomas writing together – and for sub-Costello lyrics you really couldn't beat the Thomases, gems like 'the way is all uphill she's so inclined' (from 'Slow Patience') illustrating the depth of their talents. Vocals and guitars, incidentally, were credited to the band as a whole; as Stiff Tour spectators might recall, Pete Thomas could add guitar to his many percussive talents.

Perhaps the closest parallel to 'Mad About The Rwong Boy', as the back sleeve would have it, was the first album from Squeeze before that band found its stride – onc good idea in each song struggling to catch the ear amid a sea of clichés and synthesizers. The one thing that, predictably, couldn't be faulted was the musicianship, but it really wasn't enough. And though Steve, Bruce and Pete donned Sixties togs for the high-camp sleeve photo, they contrived to produce a typically empty and directionless early-Eighties record. Like The Rumour before them, the loss of a supremely gifted singer/songwriter proved too much of a load to spread around. No, they were clearly mad to have recorded *without* the boy – and he couldn't come back too soon…

Meanwhile, back in the States, Columbia Records executives were scratching their heads and wondering what the "mad Limey with the glasses" was going to do next. In an industry where acts are defined only as successes or failures, Costello seemed intent at times on walking the dividing line. When the guy played US dates his album fell out of the charts; when he stayed home, his next album went Top Twenty just the same – and that after more than a year between releases. Hell, he was even more unpredictable than Bruce Springsteen – and at least *he* toured.

The answer, the men on the 14th floor decided, was to compile not a 'Best Of' selection as is usual after four or five studio albums, but a 'Rest Of': a 20-track resumé of tracks unavailable in the States that included freebies, UK B-sides, singles not on albums and tracks omitted from the US long-players. There aren't too many artists whose more obscure material could stand up to such treatment – and even they might justifiably have objected to the record company taking such liberties. As it was, 'Taking Liberties' was released in the States in October 1980, receiving the F-Beat seal of approval when a matching cassette-only issue '10 Bloody Marys & 10 How's Your Fathers' appeared simultaneously in the UK.

Although 'Taking Liberties' sold well as an import in Britain, the cassette had the advantage of a revised track listing that reflected the difference in album content on both sides of the Atlantic. It was the most attractively packaged Costello cassette yet, with full personnel and recording details on an embossed sleeve, and both cassette and library case were finished in a fetching shade of gold.

The contents of both compilations included some Elvis gold, too, in the likes of 'Detectives' and 'Radio Radio', together with some hitherto buried treasures in 'Big Tears' and 'Tiny Steps', the best of the B-sides. Talking of flips, the Flip City influence of 'Radio Sweetheart', the track that once backed 'Less Than Zero', was worthy of wider exposure than it enjoyed at the time of release. Stiff's habit of swiftly deleting singles (and Radar's habit of giving them away) created any number of collectors' items, thus ensuring that one or other of these late-1980 releases would be top of every self-respecting Costello fan's Christmas list.

The collection succeeded in achieving what many 'Greatest Hits' packages, for all their grandiose intentions, fail to do: giving an idea of the breadth and scope of the songwriter and musicians involved. What was more, the tracks held together well enough to avoid sounding like a TV-advertised compilation. And if it wasn't gold all the way, even the base metal of something like 'Crawling To The USA' had a certain sparkle. The song – a phrase from which he had titled 'Taking Liberties' – was recorded at Waterloo Studios, Sydney, Australia in late 1978 and brought Elvis a bit part in 'Americathon', a rock'n'roll teen exploitation pic, the following year. If the film hadn't been worth sitting through to see a newly-ennobled Costello (now Lord Manchester – good grief, couldn't the Yanks get *anything* right?) miming to the aforementioned song live in London, at least his fans didn't have to buy the wretched soundtrack to obtain that elusive two minutes 52…

Having regained his zest for the pulsating world of pop, what was Elvis going to do with it? The answer was to return to the common denominator of his four varied albums to date and produce a collection of songs that re-established his right to be considered one of the major songwriters of the post-punk era, or indeed of *any* era. Taking the best elements of past work – the lyrical zest of his debut album, the energy of 'This Year's Model', the commerciality of

'Armed Forces' – he fashioned a selection of instant Greatest Hits entitled 'Trust' that was a reaffirmation of his fans' faith in Costello the complete pop performer.

And with this concentration on form, the art of the three-minute statement, came the realisation that – hell, this guy could *sing*. He was taking more chances, doing the simple things better, hitting all the right notes with a conviction whose absence had previously been buried inconspicuously in the mix. 'Shot With His Own Gun', soon to become a live set opener, was a case in point: a dramatic pianoforte accompaniment from the classically trained Nieve provided the sole counterpoint to one of Costello's best vocals on record.

Just as surely as 'My Aim Is True' was the work of a solo singer-songwriter, so 'Trust' represented the best evidence yet that Costello and The Attractions were indeed a *group*. That much was obvious from the way 'Clubland', the opening track, got straight down to business. Unusually it included a couple of bursts of Who-like feedback guitar, but very controlled as if to underline a point; very little extraneous instrumentation could be found in any of the songs. Lyrically, 'Clubland's' clever encapsulation of some of the seamier aspects of society threatened to win Costello the accolade of 'Britain's Tom Waits': each and every line bursting with meaning and double meaning, offering more shades of interpretation than many complete songs by lesser yet still much-heralded talents.

Yet none of the album's tracks, with the exception of the jokey 'Fish And Chip Paper', ever became clever-clever. Though it was no 20-track epic this time, 'Trust' offered 14 songs of far greater breadth than its predecessor: from the country couplets of 'Different Finger' to the echo-laden rockabilly of 'Luxembourg' with its John Lennonish fade, from the Bo Diddley drums of 'Lovers Walk' to the piano-and-vocal *tour de force* of 'Shot With His Own Gun', this was a real palace of varieties.

Musically, the key to the album was Bruce Thomas' muscular bass work which added substance and appeared like an extra vocal line on the Squeeze-ish 'Pretty Words'. A new-found confidence ran through the writing and playing: such an accusatory title as 'You'll Never Be A Man' had to be delivered from a position of strength – and The Attractions had the muscle to back up every threat from Costello's pen. And menace hadn't gone out of fashion, not by a long chalk. 'White Knuckles' reopened the 'Elvis Costello as misogynist' controversy, but its flat, documentary tone suggested he'd come a long way since the days of 'Wave A White Flag'; there he'd been doing the neck-wringing while here he plays the observer/agony aunt. "You don't have to take it," he advises – and you realise he might just have been listening to his critics after all.

Freed from his soul straitjacket, Steve Nieve was clearly enjoying his new-found freedom to play piano as well as organ, punctuating the songs with some impressive pianoforte. He turned to organ for the brooding, intense 'Watch Your Step', a song that easily equalled anything on 'Get Happy..' for sheer unadulterated soul, while 'Different Finger's' tragi-comic tale of marital infidelity in a hotel room made a fitting companion to Flip City's 'Flatfoot Hotel' and the last album's 'Motel Matches' in Elvis' collection of roadhouse laments.

'Big Sister's Clothes', an engaging piece of typical wordplay set to a simple yet effective stop-start melody, was a track that rightly received much attention from the press critics. Strangely enough, it was the one track on the album Nick Lowe "wasn't to blame for" producing, as a tiny label footnote put it. It was also a much-overdubbed demo track that Costello completed entirely on his own, in the fashion of the previous album's 'New Amsterdam'. And, as one in the eye for those who sought to analyse the 'progression' in his songwriting from the early days, he was pleased to point out in 1984 that although "the critics believed that it was in this song that I evolved into a mature songwriter…I wrote the song more than eight years ago."

There were two occasions on 'Trust' when Elvis put his foot down to remind listeners that he still had the speed to leave all opposition dawdling in his wake. The first was the aforementioned 'Luxembourg', a hot slice of raw rock hidden away on side one, the second was 'From A Whisper To A Scream' featuring joint lead vocals from Squeeze's Glenn Tilbrook and the thrashing guitar style of honorary Attraction Martin Belmont. Though Belmont's scything rhythm chords suited the song admirably, it was clear that had his talents been added to the line up on a full-time basis several degrees of subtlety would have been lost. It was hard to believe that the full-tilt rock'n'roll band of this track had been responsible for the precise, poignant and perfectly memorable 'New Lace Sleeves' that preceded it, or indeed the country-flavoured 'Different Finger' that followed. But that, as Jake Riviera might have sloganised, was the attraction of The Attractions – jacks of all trades and masters, it seemed, of many.

Yes, there was something for everyone on 'Trust', and it was nothing less than scandalous that a larger section of the British public didn't take it to their hearts. Compared with the packaging gimmicks of 'Armed Forces' and to a lesser extent 'Get Happy..' the wrapper was plain and unostentatious: the monochrome Costello on the inner sleeve in overcoat, shades and broad-brimmed hat lighting a cigarette offered the listener something it was becoming ever more difficult to find – *intelligent* pop music.

Squeeze, of course, were an act with that self-same aim who also suffered from an excess of critical acclaim over sales. So with Jake Riviera taking an interest, it was no surprise to find them touring the US with The Attractions in early 1981. The 'English Mugs' tour of January and February provided more than just an opportunity for Costello and Glenn Tilbrook to encore with 'From A Whisper To A Scream'; it gave both sides a chance to observe and learn from each other. Elvis co-headlined with Talking Heads and Tom Petty on one of their earlier visits to the States, but never faced a nightly challenge from what was rightly regarded as one of the most talented young British bands for quite some while.

Squeeze were reasonably well known in their own right, having been employed by Miles Copeland as advance guard for The Police in pioneering the low-cost, small-stage tour that not only broke Sting and Co. but was copied by almost every British band to break in the States before the advent of MTV. This was to be their best yet. "The venues were well-chosen, the itinerary was well worked out and both bands complemented each other well," commented Tilbrook. As if to emphasise the fact, Elvis was contracted with Roger Bechirian to produce the band's next album, to be recorded on their return.

The album was 'East Side Story', released some four months after 'Trust' in May, and there were definite parallels between the two records – for in the same way as Costello had exhibited his own mastery of an impressive variety of styles, he helped Squeeze break away from the successful sound and style established over their last two albums with former producer John Wood to explore new and exciting directions. And the result was acclaimed by the critics as a roaring success. "This is state of the art pop music," proclaimed *NME* in an enthusiastic review typical of the press as a whole.

One of Costello's aces in the reshuffled Squeeze pack was Jools Holland's replacement, ex-Ace keyboardist Paul Carrack. Though recruited primarily for his abilities at the ivories, his voice, Elvis recalled, was one of the most soulful to be found in British rock – and with two vocalists already in the group it was unlikely to be overexposed. Carrack was given his head on 'Tempted', a Tilbrook-Difford song slowed down, re-arranged and supplied with Motown-style backing vocals courtesy of the band and Elvis himself. The result was a surprisingly mature piece of contemporary pop a few thousand light years away from 'Cool For Cats' and the other lighthearted ditties with which Squeeze had originally made their name.

Not that 'East Side Story' lacked humour. 'Piccadilly' continued the band's time-honoured 'all boys together' theme, but was now only one strand of a fascinating tapestry. There was a departure for them in the shape of a country-flavoured song, 'Labelled With Love', which when extracted as a single made number 4 – considerably better than their producer's own chart performance of late. But whether observing life with a wry insight ('Woman's World') or analysing relationships ('Someone Else's Heart'), lyricist/rhythm guitarist Chris Difford fully justified Costello's high opinion of him as one of British rock's worthier wordsmiths.

Though comparisons are invidious, the 14 tracks on Squeeze's effort bore the closest comparisons with those of their producer. And if the tracks offered a manifesto of the different styles of which the band were capable, they were unfortunate that in selecting the white soul direction of 'Tempted' for their next, self-produced, album they failed to sustain the interest they'd inspired under Costello's direction. To be fair, they couldn't have been helped by an abrupt and unexplained break with Jake Riviera's management and the loss of Paul Carrack to F-Beat signing Carlene Carter's band. And the proposed employment of Carlene's fiancé Nick Lowe as producer for the next album fell through, even though they'd finished demos. Little surprise, then, that the album in question, 'Sweets From A Stranger', turned out to be their last. It was a sweet, strange irony too that sharing backing vocals with Elvis on that record's one standout track, 'Black Coffee In Bed', was Paul Young – a singer who, a year later and after Squeeze had disbanded, took the style to a successful and profitable conclusion with his 'No Parlez' album.

Squeeze foundered in the no-man's land between their teen audience, eager for a glimpse of pretty-boy Glenn Tilbrook and eager to pogo to a dozen variations on the 'Cool For Cats' theme, and the critics whose 'new Lennon and McCartney' tag ultimately failed to win them a more mature audience of the size they deserved. In that respect, their involvement with Costello sowed the seeds of destruction by deviating from the tried-and-tested formula of 'Cool For Cats' and 'Argy Bargy'. Yet Elvis himself still seemed able to take a hard-core of dedicated fans through the many changes his music had undergone since the early days.

In the comparatively fickle singles market, though, his fortunes seemed to be in decline. 'Clubland', released in December for the pre-Christmas market, fared less than festively in reaching only number 60 despite the bonus of two previously hard-to-find songs on the flip. Though a classic Costello track, it had hardly been the obvious single – and the same could be said for 'Watch Your Step', the American choice; perhaps Jake wanted Elvis on 'Soul Train'. But when 'From A Whisper To A Scream' failed even to register a chart placing at all in February 1981 – despite a British TV appearance on the 'Jim'll Fix It' show to let a young fan become a roadie for a day – it marked Costello's chart nadir by becoming the first

outright flop since 'Red Shoes' back in July 1977, nearly four years
previously.

Elvis' British tour of March 1981, 'A Tour To Trust', was an
up-and-down affair. With a support act he'd brought over from
Sweden called Dave and The Mistakes who looked and sounded
like a third-rate Meatloaf, Costello had little competition to contend
with except his own pride. At London's Rainbow Theatre, a near
full-house of rabid Costellophiles saw him open with 'Shot With His
Own Gun' (complete with overcoat and cigarette) and add such
delights as a silky version of Randy Crawford's 'One Day I'll Fly
Away' to a varied set. In Birmingham, though, the audience was
somewhat less attentive and consequently paid the penalty: bored
with 'Get Happy..' and 'Trust' material, they wanted the hits which,
Elvis promised, would come at the end. There were no encores.

It was plain that while a nucleus of loyal fans remained, he'd
all but lost the commercial momentum imparted by 'Armed
Forces'. As the tour headed homeward to West London, the
question was – which way now?

Elvis had clearly reached a turning point in his career. He'd
been launched amid a welter of hype and smart marketing, yet
proved himself an enduring talent by following up his first album of
memorable songs with an uncompromising second set which
knocked the critics sideways. A massive hit single had brought his
music to many who had previously considered him too loud, aggressive or just plain overbearing, and ensured that his music was aired
on the radio in heavy rotation. Two years and a couple of albums on,
though, that was no longer the case: Costello was a known quanti-
ty, not yet a 'golden oldie' with nostalgia appeal, yet certainly more
than a touch passé by comparison with the New Romantics and
synthesizer duos currently invading both charts and airwaves. He
was aware of the situation, make no mistake: he'd even considered
reverting to his own name since, "There is a possibility that you can
get tied to a time, in people's minds; people associate us and The
Buzzcocks and The Clash with 1978."

The answer to the dilemma came in the shape of an album,
'Almost Blue', released only nine months after 'Trust' in October
1981. That the record consisted entirely of cover versions was
enough of a surprise; what came as more of a shock to fans and
critics alike was the fact that these were no ordinary songs – they
were *country* songs…

Nashville Cat

Elvis' motivation to record an album of country music was sincere enough; as anyone who'd followed his career from Flip City days would have known, his love of the music was undoubted. But until July 1978, when he worked with George Jones in Nashville, he never considered the idea as anything more than a wild fantasy. The suggestion that Jones record 'Stranger In The House' was made not by its bashful author but by Greg Geller, the man responsible for signing Costello to Columbia in the States: Elvis himself admitted that he would "never have had the guts to do something like that". The two sang the song together and it appeared on an album of duets Jones released in 1979. And, though for some strange reason the chair marked 'Costello' among the contributors' personalised seats on the cover of 'My Very Special Guests' was overturned – a comment on his iconoclastic Christian name, perhaps? – he had no reason to feel displeased with his contribution. A song that was first recorded (as 'Cheap Reward') in a Middlesex front room in 1976 had certainly brought him a long way.

The session introduced him to Billy Sherrill, Jones' long-time producer and a country-music legend in his own right. Since Costello had never worked with anyone but Nick Lowe in the studio before, dealing with the laconic Sherrill must have been something of a challenge. Yet when the producer asked Elvis to add an acoustic guitar solo to the finished recording – and Costello, despite his nerves, managed to do so – a strange kind of mutual respect sprang up between the veteran from Nashville and the strange-looking singer from England who'd written a country song. And so it was that Elvis decided, "If we are going to do a record of ballads and country music, I want to do it properly and go to the heart of it and do it with Billy Sherrill."

The key to 'Almost Blue' was Costello's infatuation with Gram Parsons – an association that went much deeper than his oft-repeated comment about the singer's early demise. "Gram

Parsons had it all sussed," he told Nick Kent. "He didn't stick around – he made his best work and then he died. That's the way I want to do it." Well this was 1981 and Costello was still here, wondering how to top a collection of his best songs to date. "I'm not going to be around to witness my artistic decline," he snarled in '77 as the payoff to his deathwish; but if he'd hit an artistic peak, it had yet to be recognised by the kind of public acclaim he deserved.

Ironically, Gram Parsons had had the same problem. He first came to prominence when he was enrolled as a Byrd by Roger McGuinn, who was to hire and fire band members with increasing regularity after the departure of David Crosby and Gene Clark, his two fellow songwriters whose talents were never adequately replaced. This was 1968, and The Byrds had done no wrong in the eyes of their audience – until, that was, Parsons encouraged them to bring country and bluegrass into their repertoire where once folk had provided the source material for their – in all senses – electric music.

In the years since its release, 'Sweetheart Of The Rodeo' has been acclaimed as a ground-breaking album – but at the time it was poorly received by a rock audience for whom country lacked sophistication and excitement. Parsons' subsequent adventures with The Flying Burrito Brothers gained him little fame, especially in comparison with his shortlived dalliance with The Rolling Stones and their entourage. After a two-year break, he recommenced his solo career in 1973 with the 'GP' album, but his next release was to be posthumous; an overdose of morphine and alcohol ended his life at the age of 26 – coincidentally, Costello's own age at the time of the 'Almost Blue' recording.

Despite this fixation with Parsons' tragic demise – which took a twist as macabre as the darkest Costello song when two friends kidnapped and cremated his body in the desert in a bizarre deathwish pact – Elvis' affection for Gram's type of country was evident in much of his earlier material. 'Radio Sweetheart', the first B-side with Clover, and 'Stranger In The House' from the same sessions put his cards on the table – and if no less a figure than George Jones picked up on the latter, well maybe it was worth a gamble after all. For the rest of The Attractions it was just as much of an adventure; when Bruce Thomas sang in 1971 about 'funky country music all night long', he surely didn't imagine that 10 years later he'd be recording in Nashville.

Comparing the performance of 'Get Happy..' with its successor – a 14-week chart stay which peaked at number 2 as against seven weeks and a number 9 best position – a cynic might comment that originality would appear to count for little. Costello's contention that a country album "would probably reach a lot of people that don't buy our records normally" couldn't be faulted, and made commercial sense. His counter-proposal, that it would also reach "a lot of people who never listen to country records" was open to debate – unless he meant his own fans. Just how tongue-in-cheek *was* the sticker on the record sleeve warning "narrow minded people" that country music could "produce a radical reaction"? Whatever his true feelings, perhaps it was Elvis' growing confidence in his singing that prompted him to tackle a set of other people's songs; in any case, he proclaimed himself "totally bored" with his own music, 'Trust' having been "under realised…we didn't follow it through to anything definite enough."

Nothing could be more definite than Costello's choice of venue – Nashville, Tennessee, Music City itself. For producer he chose Billy Sherrill, while to complete the band he once more employed the services of Clover's lead guitarist John McFee. "We wanted the sound," said Elvis, "but we didn't necessarily want the main instrumental line which usually comes from the steel in country to be somebody we'd never heard before."

Now a fully-fledged member of Adult Oriented Rockstars The Doobie Brothers, McFee couldn't have needed the bucks, yet he was happy to renew his association with Costello and company. It wasn't the first time they'd linked up on McFee's home territory; a date at the Palomino Club in Los Angeles in February 1979 saw him join The Attractions for a gallop through such country classics as Jim Reeves' 'He'll Have To Go', George Jones' '(If I Could Put Them All Together) I'd Have You' and Eddie Noack's bizarre 'Psycho'. So when the 'Elvis Costello Quintet' mustered in CBS Studio A, Nashville, on 18 May 1981 few introductions were needed.

If Sherrill's track record earned Costello's respect, the singer was nevertheless definite in his intention to arrange the songs himself; indeed, one of the advantages of recruiting John McFee was "so we could do the arrangements properly before we got to Nashville so there wouldn't be too much of an outside influence on the way the songs went." This attitude was somewhat surprising, since the accepted country music relationship between producer and artist is something of a dictatorship; the producer often selects the material, supervises the arrangements and invariably includes one of his own compositions on the record.

The wily Sherrill did indeed include one of his songs, 'Too Far Gone', on the album, while string and choral overdubs added to 'sweeten' the basic tracks after recording helped redress the balance of arrangements more than somewhat – but even so, it was to be a long way from an everyday Nashville session. In retrospect, Elvis confessed that he was a little in awe of the veteran producer, but the ice thawed perceptibly when The Attractions nervously unveiled their 100 miles-a-minute version of 'Why Don't You Love

Me (Like You Used To Do)' which was to open side one at a lick. "We thought it might be walking on hallowed ground a bit", remarked Costello. "We were expecting him to walk out." Instead, as the mastertape faded to silence and the band awaited a verdict in the studio, the control-room intercom crackled loudly. "Elvis," drawled Sherrill, "we got Hank Williams on the 'phone."

From then on it was smiles all round. The band started with 30 songs, almost all country classics, and were to record an astounding 25 of those in only five days, working from two in the afternoon to eight in the evening, before picking the best dozen. "The best way to work was not to labour over a song," Costello explained. "If it didn't come in one or two takes we'd go on to another song." Their producer was familiar with all but the two Gram Parsons songs and the stage favourite 'Psycho', which Costello considered including but eventually rejected as "a gimmick". Yet Sherrill still couldn't understand the motivation behind the project. "He found it quite hard to adjust to why all these mad English people were so enthusiastic about those songs which were old hat to him," the singer noted.

So what *was* Costello's reasoning in coming to Nashville to record? After all, a British country and western album is just as pointless an exercise in some people's eyes whether it's made out in Tennessee or wild West London... Even though Elvis found it impossible to give Billy Sherrill complete control, he clearly believed that the Nashville sound was worth a certain amount of time and trouble to obtain. Perhaps more important, though, was his enthusiasm for fulfilling a dream, recording at the home and heart of country music – but *on his own terms*. Self-indulgent the result might have seemed to some, but it was one occasion in which Elvis Costello the artist and Declan McManus the fan were briefly united.

In a break from Nashville tradition 'Almost Blue' offered six tracks a side – one more than the standard ration. And if Costello was being generous with the helpings then he could hardly have searched wider in the country cookbook to find an appetising selection of songs. But fair warning was served by their breakneck reading of 'Why Don't You Love Me (Like You Used To Do)' which seemed to signal The Attractions' intention to throw undue reverence out of the studio door. As an opening track, though, it wasn't really representative of the record's overall content – as Costello commented, "the meat of the album is the ballads." So if any country purists had ripped stylus from vinyl after the mere 90 seconds of that iconoclastic opening blast, then they'd have missed a treat.

Costello's treatment of 'Sweet Dreams' was heavily influenced by the cover of the song on 'Roy Orbison Sings Don Gibson', a mellow, vibraphone-embellished stroll through one of country's more enduring standards by one of pop's great voices. Though Patsy Cline and Loretta Lynn of country's female faction had cut it, too, it was the "R&B feel" of Orbison's version that attracted Elvis to the song. And although any grit in his own reading was to be successfully obscured by the lush backing vocals supplied by Nashville Edition and overdubbed later by Sherrill, it was a creditable attempt.

Talking of Loretta Lynn, it was her repertoire that attracted ivory-tickling Attraction Steve Nieve to 'Success', another side one song. The thrust of the lyric – "Success has made a failure of our home" – was doubtless not lost on a singer who had problems in that field himself not so long ago.

Gram Parsons' two contributions to 'Almost Blue' fittingly inspired Costello's most heartfelt vocals. 'I'm Your Toy' was the retitled 'Hot Burrito No. 1' from the Burrito Brothers' first album 'The Gilded Palace Of Sin', while 'How Much I Lied', with which Elvis chose to close the album, came from Parsons' 'GP' set. Whether it was familiarity, affection or the fact that there was no Nashville yardstick for his producer to measure him against, the singer's performances were looser and less formal than on most of the selections, and all the better for it. Nieve's piano-work on 'How Much I Lied' – recorded in one take – was also especially commendable.

As previously mentioned, the Parsons tracks were the only selections to make an album that waved the flag for contemporary country. Most of the others dated back some years, like Merle Haggard's 'Tonight The Bottle Let Me Down', attacked in chirpily aggressive uptempo fashion, and the Charlie Rich classic 'Sitting' And Thinkin''. In Costello's view, Rich was "one of the most versatile and perhaps even the most talented of all the people on Sun", the Memphis record label that had given Elvis' namesake his first break back in 1954. To tie things in still further, Billy Sherrill engineered Rich's original recording of the song on Sun and was the producer when Rich remade the track 15 years later for Epic – a happy coincidence indeed. At one point, Costello wanted to leave this song off the album, commenting that he sounded "a bit like Dean Martin", but eventually changed his mind when he "gradually got used to the fact that I was maybe a modern Dean Martin."

Sherrill's own 'Too Far Gone', first recorded by Tammy Wynette and George Jones on their 'We Go Together' album, was one of only three songs on the album to break the three-minute barrier. One of the others, 'Good Year For The Roses', was also a George Jones song and was selected as the first single as well as starting side two. With piping organ from Steve Nieve trying hard to surface over the massed vocals and strings, both tracks were heavily over-produced ballads in the country tradition – yet every so often you could hear The Attractions fighting to get out.

'Almost Blue' was packaged with the by-now typical lack of ostentation, its sleeve borrowing liberally from jazzman Kenny Burrell's 'Midnight Blue' in its typographical content. If this tied it in with the smoky ambience of 'Trust' its sales were soon to surpass those of its predecessor, the sarcastic peel-off warning notice being replaced by a more usual 'Contains the Hit Singles…' sticker. The sticker also remedied a hitherto unnoticed deficiency in the sleeve design by announcing the artist's name; Costello's removal of the trademark hornrims combined with the overprinting of the album's title had obviously confused some retailers. Not so his British fans, though – they bought it in droves, sending the album to number 7 in the UK charts. The catalyst for this success was 'Good Year For The Roses', released as a single in September. By the time of the album's release the following month 'Roses' nestled snugly at number 6 – a freak hit, perhaps, but gaining from simultaneous exposure on both the pop-oriented Radio 1 and the MOR Radio 2 channel.

If the album seems as artistically meaningless now as it did then, it's possibly because that was its very intention. Certainly, it had relieved Elvis of the immediate problem of following the artistic *tour de force* that was 'Trust', yet it was nothing to be ashamed of: a release under another name, for example, might have teased the critics but honour would scarcely have been satisfied. And its long-term effect on Costello's music has been negligible; his command of the country lyric idiom was already more than proved by songs like 'Stranger' and 'Trust's 'Different Finger', while as far as performance went there was little in the execution of 'Almost Blue' that was to be reflected in later work. Indeed, comparing the new album's almost stately reading of the Johnny Burnette/Rock 'n' Roll Trio's rockabilly classic 'Honey Hush' with 'Trust's' self-penned 'Luxembourg' was nothing less than revelatory. No, if country artists made a habit of recording 'tribute' albums then this was Elvis Costello's tribute to Nashville, no more no less.
Buoyed by the success of single and album, an extension of Costello's country capers was swiftly scheduled in the shape of a New Year's show at London's Royal Albert Hall on 7 January 1982 with the 92-piece Royal Philharmonic Orchestra in attendance. The material essayed by the somewhat unwieldy ensemble took in selected numbers from the Costello songbook to add to his country repertoire, with orchestrator Robert Kirby (who had also worked with the Strawbs) providing the string arrangements.

Although the Albert Hall gig was a one-off in terms of the 'added Attractions', it was in fact one of the only nine dates to comprise the Almost Blue World Tour that took in London, Los

Angeles, New York, Paris, Dublin and Nashville. But this was the big one – and if Costello showed his nerves in botching the opening verse of 'Shot With His Own Gun', the song that opened the second (orchestral) set, he had good reason to. "We'd done one rehearsal the day before and I hadn't heard the arrangements before that. Robert Kirby…did them while we were away playing America over Christmas. We came back and did the rehearsal the day before and then a dress rehearsal."

Things improved after a shaky start, however, with old favourites like 'Alison' and 'Watching The Detectives' receiving orchestral assistance along with the country material the gig was designed to showcase. One new original song to turn up was 'Town Crier', a melancholy lament whose lachrymose string arrangement suited it so well that it was to appear in substantially similar form on the next album. The encore was 'Peace Love And Understanding', for which Elvis demanded its composer Nick Lowe, who was in the 6000-strong audience, stand up and take a bow. When Lowe had written the song for the Brinsleys to record way back in 1974, he could hardly have thought it would come to this.

Reviews of the concert were highly favourable, suggesting that most critics appreciated the risk Costello took in staging the event. It even seemed possible that The Attractions could tour with a scaled-down string ensemble to take the orchestral 'Almost Blue' to a yet wider audience. By this time, though, the relative failure of 'Sweet Dreams' to emulate the singles success of 'Roses' (it reached only number 42) suggested the end of the country road. The show was filmed – the footage has yet to surface – and, when the orchestrated version of 'I'm Your Toy' failed by one place to reach the UK Top Fifty in April plans for the release of a live album of the concert were quietly dropped.

That said, Costellophiles were typically well served with regard to flip-sides. Nashville out-takes appeared on the B-side of 'Roses' ('Your Angel Steps Out Of Heaven') and 'I'm Your Toy' ('Cry Cry Cry' and 'Wondering'), while the 12-inch version of the latter doubled the country quota by adding 'My Shoes Keep Walking Back To You', featuring session fiddle-player Tommy Miller, 'Blues Keep Calling' and 'Honky Tonk Girl' to the collection. The odd flip out was 'Sweet Dreams', which provided the only legitimate release for a track from the much-bootlegged Palomino concert of 1979 in 'Psycho'. Evidently, though Elvis hadn't wanted to record another version of the song, he had no qualms about letting this much-overdubbed live snippet reach the record collections of his eager fans.

When asked why he hadn't included any of his own compositions on the album, Costello commented, "The concept was to record some of the best country songs – mine don't belong to those." Despite such self-deprecating words, one of his compositions, 'Tears Before Bedtime', *had* actually been recorded but remained (with Hank Williams' 'Your Cheating Heart') one of the two unreleased tracks from the session. "People might have presumed," he said, "that I thought I was as good a songwriter as Don Gibson if I put my songs next to 'Sweet Dreams'…I know where my limits lie." If that was perhaps a wise decision, 'Almost Blue' had undoubtedly seen him push his limits that much further.

Maybe the last words on the country album and its aftermath should come from Costello himself. "I used to be quite a bigot," he commented after returning from the recording sessions, "but I tried to find things in all kinds of music that I like." Two years on, though, he found 'Almost Blue' far from easy listening. "I listen to that record now and think God. I was never *this* depressed, was I?" If anyone's 'musical bigotry' was vanquished by Elvis' fortnight in Nashville, then that was probably justification enough for the project.

Elvis Turns Emperor

Though 'Almost Blue' arguably helped widen both Costello's home market and (even more arguably) the minds of his fans, all evidence suggests that his standing in the United States had now fallen to its lowest ebb yet. 'Taking Liberties' performed very well for a collection of outtakes and rarities in reaching number 28, but the appearance of 'Trust' only a few months later saw an improvement on that showing of only two places, and 'Almost Blue', despite being made in the USA, was the last straw in a country where country music, like black music, has always been compartmentalised and segregated from the lucrative popular mainstream. Besides, the American record-buyer, it could (and has been) argued, wants to know it's getting a Bruce Springsteen album inside a Bruce Springsteen cover, as that very artist discovered when he recorded 'Nebraska', an album of acoustic 'demo-quality' compositions, an action that gave mighty Columbia a corporate coronary. And besides, who did this crazy Englishman think he was playin' redneck music anyhow?

Whatever the commercial merits and demerits of the move – and Costello has never been noted for worrying about such matters – one satisfactory side-effect of recording an album's worth of non-originals was the satisfyingly substantial selection of songs now in his pocket. To show he had no intention of keeping them there, he led The Attractions into London's AIR Studios just before Christmas of 1981, when most artists' minds would have been on the forthcoming Albert Hall audio-visual extravaganza, to commit some new songs to tape. And if the Sherrill sessions broke the mould of previous albums, it was fascinating to note that it wasn't only the venue that was different – Nick Lowe was nowhere to be seen. After six studio albums, Elvis Costello now decided to produce himself.

The pre-Christmas week that saw Costello and band take a score of new songs down to a West Country cottage in echoes of 1977 not only allowed them to get away from it all but was to put them firmly back in the rock mainstream. It was also to presage a frantic spell of live activity on both sides of the Atlantic; things had never quite been the same on the touring front since the mad days of 1979, but the new album was to be assiduously promoted nevertheless.

But first the recording which, as stated, took place at George Martin's AIR Studios in the West End. Although the label credits read 'Produced by Geoff Emerick from an original idea by Elvis Costello', the album was in reality co-produced by the two individuals concerned, Emerick being George Martin's one-time engineer. It seemed the ideal combination: a man whose experience in sound recording dated back to The Beatles and an artist himself searching for the elusive ingredient to revitalise his commercial standing. Away from Nick Lowe's familiar guiding hand, it was always on the cards that this album would take longer than its predecessors to record; with no fewer than 15 of the original 20 tracks surviving the West Country woodshedding, long hours seemed even more likely. The end result of Costello's co-production, which saw him scurrying between studio and mixing desk, was a very real change in the structure of several songs during their recording – the first time he'd rewritten material in the studio. The results were mixed.

'Imperial Bedroom' finally saw the light of day in July to critical fanfares from all sides. And it was the Americans, eager to make a Beatle connection and announcing the album as some kind of successor to 'Sgt. Pepper', who went overboard to take Elvis once more to their heaving national bosom. No-one could say that Costello, the prodigal, didn't milk it for all it was worth: *Rolling Stone* got an interview, while those media men unfortunate enough to miss out were consoled with a double-album entitled 'A Conversation With Elvis Costello' which contained lengthy interviews interspersed with music.

For avid Costello fans, all this was somewhat unnecessary. The mere fact that artist and label had broken with tradition by spreading his lyrics higgledy-piggledy over the inner bag (and one side of the label) confirmed the suspicion that this was one album that Took Itself Seriously. Significantly, although 'Imperial Bedroom' is disliked by many enthusiasts, those less conversant with Costello's music find it one of his more attractive records. As for the participants themselves, it is rumoured that Pete Thomas was less than happy with the relegation of his drums to an unusually subordinate role; indeed, one commentator went so far as to claim that he had been banned from the studio.

Whatever the truth, the result from this side of the stereo speakers sounded like the schoolboy who had the pick of the sweetshop. While 'The Specials' had seen him triumph in assisting an undisciplined nine-piece line-up to make sense of songs and transfer them to vinyl, the process was simple and uncomplicated. Squeeze already had their sound, which Elvis took delight in re-arranging to provide something distinctively different. But all that time in the control room gave Elvis a false perspective, it seemed. He was about to produce the album he thought the public would want, the definitive Elvis Costello album. For the first time, he was second guessing.

That's not to say 'Imperial Bedroom' was completely without merit – far from it. It's just that the songs with something to offer had to fight particularly hard to break through the surface, highlighting the all too frequently unrecognised benefits of Nick Lowe's straightforward production skills. Too often the match in styles between lyrics and music – a uniform success with 'East Side Story' – was imperfectly made. 'Tears Before Bedtime', for example, existed in at least four versions, including the country treatment recorded during the 'Almost Blue' sessions. After a rock 'n' roll take and a Fats Domino-style arrangement that Costello claimed "sounded like John Lennon's 'Starting Over'", the decision was made to go with a 'Tempted'-style white soul feel. Unlike 'Tears Of A Clown', 'Tracks Of My Tears' and countless other soul tearjerkers it didn't quite come off. Nonetheless, it would have been fun to hear an EP of the outtakes. Another song cut more than once was 'Man Out Of Time' – and, in typically economic fashion, Elvis spliced a couple of excerpts from a faster version onto the album track "to make it sound more exciting"; hence the manic, clattering guitar that introduces and ends the song.

Two numbers were fashioned for outside lyricists; 'Long Honeymoon' started out as a piano instrumental he'd sent to veteran Broadway lyricist Sammy Cahn (author of 'The Tender Trap', 'Come Fly With Me' and sundry others). Failing to receive any *bon mots*, he wrote the words himself but found little inspiration. The music to 'Boy With A Problem' made the slightly less tortuous journey to the South-East London residence of Squeeze wordsmith Chris Difford to find a far more satisfactory set of lyrics. This was the last track to be included on the album, The Attractions having recorded the backing one night when Elvis was out of the studio. Having lost interest in it meanwhile, he listened to it again on the final afternoon and decided he liked it enough to add a vocal (but no guitar) to it.

Perhaps the most irritating aspect of the album as a whole was the treatment of Costello's voice which swooped from speaker to speaker (as on 'Beyond Belief') quite disorientatingly – surprising for a man who in performance was accompanied vocally only by Bruce Thomas or not at all. If 'Trust' unveiled a newly confident vocalist, this was perhaps taking talent too far.

'Beyond Belief' was an example of the trouble Costello was

taking over his vocals, which, together with instrumental overdubs, took him fully three weeks to complete. When The Attractions finished recording the backing track, the song was entitled
'Land Of Give And Take'. Feeling the number was being 'thrown
away', Costello halved the lyrics, changed the title-cum-chorus and
ended up with a completely different song with an elaborate vocal
arrangement. The idea of using overlapping vocals and differing
styles was, said Costello, an attempt "to suggest there was more
than one attitude going on inside the songs." Yet this approach
could be taken to extremes, and 'Kid About It' found him singing in
what he later admitted was "an entirely unsuitable octave".

Where Costello wasn't crooning in multi-track, Steve Nieve
was filling in the blanks. From the Beatlesque string and horn
arrangements of 'And In Every Home' to the Mike Barson/
Madness-style piano of 'The Loved One', Steve dominated the
instrumental backing in a way never previously heard or needed.
And where the guitar became audible it was either phased and
flatulent (as on 'Shabby Doll') or flamenco (the Spanish-style solo of
'Pidgin English'). Perhaps the guitarist had his hands full with the
fader controls…

There was a good deal of instrumental experimentation –
Elvis playcd organ and vibes on 'Kid About It', while Steve played
the distorted guitar in the fade of 'Tears Before Bedtime' as "a
joke". Whether or not it was intended to make a point about the way
the album was being put together the newly elevated producer
liked it so much he kept it. Horns made their first (but far from their
last) appearance on a Costello record as did a mellotron, the
keyboard string simulator beloved of The Moody Blues.

Lyrically the range of ideas expressed was typically diverse:
'You Little Fool' was conceived as "one step from 'Mother's Little
Helper' by The Rolling Stones – when they were a good group" and
recorded as a suitably Catholic reprimand to liberal parenthood.
'Pidgin English', meanwhile, bemoaned the misuse of language,
especially by the newpapers and which, said Costello, could lead to
manipulation "because they've taken away your ability to say anything different." 'Shabby Doll' was inspired on tour by a framed
music-hall poster in a hotel room, while 'And In Every Home' dealt
with the problem of unemployment in a cleverly original and unpat-
ronising way. But by letting Steve run riot with the strings and
horns on the number he took the risk of losing the meaning: hence
the importance of that lyric sheet.

Like many of its predecessors, 'Imperial Bedroom' had at
least one different title during its manufacture. Perhaps the most
bizarre was 'Revolution Of The Mind', suggested by a line from
'King Heroin', an anti-drug anthem from soul superstar James
Brown. When it suggested that, when isolated from its original

context, the phrase sounded like a Moody Blues song title, it became 'PS I Love You' – the phrase that recurs in 'The Loved Ones' and 'Pidgin English'. The final name change was necessitated by a coincidentally-titled TV-promoted compilation album of love songs – and if the phrase 'Imperial Bedroom' was meaningless, at least it was unlikely to duplicate or be duplicated. In parallel with 'Armed Forces', it could be argued that the tracks on 'Imperial Bedroom' put forward a manifesto of sex equalling power – but that was not, it seemed, what its author intended. According to Costello, the title had "just the right combination of splendour and sleeze to fit all the tracks on the album," a conclusion with which it was difficult to argue.

Although dressed impeccably – Sal Forlenza, whose work had adorned the 'New Amsterdam' EP sleeve, once again provided a cover in 'Snakecharmer And Reclining Octopus' while no less a lensman than David Bailey took the back-cover mugshots – the album only truly came to life when the music was stripped down to its basics. 'Almost Blue', a belated, bittersweet title track-but-one, utilised the now-familiar Costello-plus-keyboard formula to show the rest of the album the way home.

If this analysis of 'Imperial Bedroom' seems a trifle severe, then the chart performance of the singles taken from it bears out such comments. 'You Little Fool' landed up two places short of the Top Fifty in June, while Spectoresque harmonies aplenty couldn't save 'Man Out Of Time' (reckoned by many critics to be the strongest song on the album) from a number 58 fate one scant month later. Perhaps its B-side, 'Town Crier', would have fared better, being one of the few tracks to live up to Costello's high standards with ease. Yet its subdued and downbeat mood underlined the fact that likely 45s hardly jumped from the album – and the litmus test of the singles chart was one Elvis could not lightly ignore.

Significantly, the United States' east and west coasts were the first to play host to Elvis and The Attractions as they commenced a two-month summer tour to promote the new album in July, British dates being deferred until later in the year. It was hardly surprising then, to note the failure of the two singles taken from the album to dent the UK charts. Even though 'Imperial Bedroom' justified its scattershot pattern of styles by reaching number 6 and remaining 12 weeks in the British Top Hundred, there was more than a suspicion that the individual bullets were less penetrative than in previous years.

Having deliberately fought shy of over-promoting his country album, especially in the land of its origin, Elvis Costello appreciated that there was ground to be made up in the States. The English

Mugs tour had proved a pleasant surprise: the package of The Attractions and Squeeze was well received, while 'Trust' nudged into the Top Thirty at number 26. If he'd expected 'Almost Blue' to bring few chart honours (it reached number 48 thanks to a hard-core of fans), the summer of 1982 brought a fresh challenge. Would Costello take the media bull by the horns?

The answer was yes, though some blood was spilled in the process. *Rolling Stone's* previously mentioned cover story, head-lined 'Elvis Costello Repents', did the job once and for all, and he has since directed his more tactless interviewers to read it, saying "I can't go on right through my life explaining that incident." It did the job; major stories in *Newsweek* and the *New York* and *Los Angeles Times* indicated the olive branch had been accepted. Elvis waved the white flag; the slate was wiped clean.

In a country that coined the term 'arena rock', Elvis was still small-time; the biggest venue he played on the '82 tour was the 12,000-capacity Forest Hills tennis stadium. But there were signs that his communication with the audience was hitting new peaks – and not just in his new-found affability. The angry, accusing stare from a motionless stance had gone, to be replaced by movement and gesticulation. On a couple of occasions in each set he even unbuckled his guitar and let his hands do the talking, underlining the deeper meaning behind 'Kid About It' and 'And In Every Home'.

There were indications, too, that The Attractions were matching slick musical moves to their frontman's new-found confi-dence. Medleys and interesting new melodies were interspersed with familiar material: Sonny Boy Williamson's 'Help Me' provided temporary relief from the tension of 'Watching The Detectives', the new ('Beyond Belief') ran into the old ('Clubland'), while in an ironic twist Ray Charles unknowingly provided the most impress-ive cover of the set in 'Danger Zone', the B-side to his 'Hit The Road Jack', written by Percy Mayfield.

But the full import of the most significant new and unre-corded song was probably lost on many Americans. A piano-based ballad with music from Clive Langer, the tenor of 'Shipbuilding' could be judged from the opening line 'Is it worth it?' – and even without Elvis' customary introduction explaining the song's inspira-tion, the recently-fought Falklands War between the United King-dom and Argentina, the sentiment could be taken to heart by a nation with the memory of countless Vietnam dead still far from faded. With the South Atlantic ceasefire only declared on 14 June, the song was prompt – perhaps *too* prompt – for even a home audience to digest just yet. Its hour had yet to come.

Elvis' choice of support for the British tour of September/October 1982 was The Bluebells, a Scottish pop five-piece who'd impressed him so much that he'd expressed interest in producing them. Although sessions for the proposed album took place late in the year while The Attractions were working on their next 'solo' long-player, both these projects failed to see release. Though The Attractions' second album remained unheard three years later, a couple of The Bluebells' collaborations with Costello *did* eventually surface as B-sides and 12-inch bonus tracks. And when the band reached the UK charts in May 1984 with 'I'm Falling', their sound was thought by many to owe more than a nod to their former mentor.

As with the summer tour of the States, this was the new, animated Costello in view. Encouraged by the audience reception of the musical medleys introduced into the American set, 'King Horse' now boasted a couple of verses of the O'Jays' 1972 Philadelphia classic 'Backstabbers', while his version of Bobby Bland's 'Two Steps From The Blues' got its first airing in England. But while home audiences were marvelling at the new-look Elvis, Rough Trade Records released a version of 'Shipbuilding' that bulleted to the top of the independent singles chart. Its singer was former Soft Machine stalwart and fellow West London resident Robert Wyatt.

This dramatic new version of the song owed much of its hymnal, stately feel to Wyatt's high-pitched, distinctively English delivery, most recently heard on a series of explicitly political releases on the 'alternative' Rough Trade label. As Elvis explained, "The melody was written by Clive with Robert in mind, so the tune really suggested Robert's voice… I just hoped the words were the sort of sentiments that he would be able to sing." The backing track winged its way around the world to allow the various participants to overdub their contributions; the full line-up read Steve Nieve (piano), Mark Bedford of Madness (bass), Martin Hughes of Clive Langer's Boxes (drums) and Langer himself on organ, with Costello chiming in on backing vocals. The production credit reflected the geographical complications inherent in such a meeting of musicians: what was more, the legend 'A Clangwinstello Production', with Langer's cohort Alan Winstanley in there somewhere, was as novel as anything Stiff dreamed up in their heyday.

'Shipbuilding' wasn't the only work Elvis Costello undertook with other artists in 1982. Apart from The Bluebells, he produced material for Australian band Mental As Anything while Down Under in the summer, at the same time as Steve Nieve was contributing to 'Shipbuilding'. And it gave him a particular thrill three months earlier to write Dusty Springfield an extra verse for 'Just A Memory', a song he recorded for the 'New Amsterdam' EP with her in mind. "I was actually on the phone to her, she was trans-atlantic, singing the new verse…and I've got the phone at arm's length incredulous that I've got Dusty Springfield singing my new verse back to me."

But if the appearance of 'Losing You', as the song was retitled, on Dusty's 'White Heat' album in December was a personal highlight of Elvis Costello's year, then 'Shipbuilding' is the song most of his fans will recall in years to come. Robert Wyatt's version, re-released the following June, made a very creditable showing in reaching the Top Forty during the year that cruise missiles arrived in Britain. Madness, U2, Fun Boy Three, The Style Council and others all made their protest in various ways but the majesty of 'Shipbuilding' remains unsurpassed.

Bold As Brass

Most Londoners were bent on completing their last-minute 1982 Christmas shopping as The Attractions' roadcrew moved into the Albert Hall, where Elvis had scheduled a brace of seasonal dates to exorcise the ghosts of the 'Almost Blue' orchestral evening. Avid Costello-watchers were quick to book their boxes – there was doubtless some significance in date, venue or both. They were rewarded with their first belated Christmas present when Elvis strolled out alone, guitar in hand, for a short solo set. The second surprise came with the appearance of a three-man horn section to accompany the lengthy encores. Since few backsides remained on the Albert Hall seats by this time (they were even boogying in the boxes) many fans were perhaps unaware of their introduction to the TKO Horns.

The trio – Scotsman Jim Paterson, Brian Maurice and Paul Speare – had lately supplied the belting brass behind Kevin Rowland's Mark II version of Dexys Midnight Runners. With their leader turning his attention from soulful saxophones to folksy fiddles, a parting of the ways saw the trio freelancing with such gigging bands as The Q-Tips (featuring solo star-to-be Paul Young) before accepting this temporary gig with The Attractions. Due to a judicious choice of encore material (a burst from 'Get Happy..' included), their addition to the ranks was adjudged to be wholly satisfactory.

Apart from the TKO Horns the Albert Hall played host to several unexpected delights – two fully-fashioned new songs in the promising 'Everyday I Write The Book' and the less immediately impressive 'Mouth Almighty', and the author's own version of 'Shipbuilding' that led neatly into 'Oliver's Army'. Even Elvis himself looked different; if your vantage point wasn't up in 'the gods', a couple of weeks' growth of stubble could be discerned from the more expensive seats.

This was a new, relaxed Costello on show – he'd even taken to returning to the stage for encores in a gorilla suit, as reviewers in the States recently reported. But though the Royal Albert Hall was too imposing a venue for Elvis to go ape, he was still quite prepared to be irreverent. A steaming 'High Fidelity' was introduced as "A song by The Kids From Fame" – the cast of that TV show having just released a single of the same name – and, coincidentally, the last pop act to play the RAH. Fame, though, is a relative concept, and the fact that Costello was driven away in a Rolls-Royce seemed to suggest that fortune, if not fame, continued to favour him despite a low profile in the singles chart. And if any shades remained of his previous Albert Hall appearance, he could glide away in the ultimate in four-wheel luxury confident that those ghosts had indisputably been busted.

When Elvis and The Attractions reconvened at Air London on 27 January after a belated Christmas break to record Costello's eighth studio album (their seventh together), it was to be with a new producer. Though the venue remained the same, Elvis' collaboration with Clive Langer on 'Shipbuilding' convinced him that the time was right to take the association further – and since the TKO Horns loomed large in his plans, it's likely that Langer's production of 'Too Rye Ay', Dexys Midnight Runners' second album released the previous August, had much to do with his reasons.

Since his last album sessions, Costello had taken two stabs at resuscitating his chart career on the singles front, but without any great success. The first, the self-produced 'From Head To Toe', was indirectly lifted from the Motown songbook and, while archivists rooting through their old Smokey Robinson albums discovered the song on the Miracles' 'Going To A Go-Go' long-player, it wasn't widely appreciated that the inspiration to record it came from a re-released series of beat-era albums on Jake Riviera's own Edsel label. The Escorts were just one of many bands of the day to look to Motown for inspiration, and it was their 1966 version he heard. The intention was to release an EP of Sixties songs, and perhaps that would have generated more interest.

As it was, 'From Head To Toe' – one of Smokey's less sensational songs – brought little out of the ordinary from singer or band and failed to make the Top Forty by three places, despite WEA taking the old 'Help Us Hype Elvis' slogan too literally and giving away free copies of 'Get Happy..' at chart return shops. Of the other projected EP tracks, 'The World Of Lonely Hearts' – written by the American team of Doc Pomus and Mort Shuman and covered in 1967 by Andy Fairweather Low's Amen Corner – made the B-side, while 'Night Time' (the B-side to the Escorts' 'Head To Toe') was to surface in 1983 as a 12-inch bonus.

If Costello's fourth 45 of 1982 was disappointing, his parting shot was nothing less than zero. 'Party Party' appeared on the

A&M label and was the title song to a movie whose soundtrack, released by the same company, boasted performances from such luminaries as Madness, Midge Ure from Ultravox and Sting from The Police. But while Sting wisely confined his contribution to covers of 'Tutti Frutti' and 'Need Your Love So Bad' (produced, incidentally, by Dave Edumunds), Elvis' attempt to come up with an original 'to order' as a title track fell as flat as the film itself. His involvement stemmed from a 40-minute pilot version which he considered "very funny…it would have made a great TV play and perhaps not such a great film." In true contradictory style, then, Elvis pinned his colours to the mast and watched both single and soundtrack dragged down by a s(t)inking film.

The track, which its author admitted was "written in ten minutes and to be honest it sounds like it", was significant in that it was Costello's first use of a horn section; Annie Whitehead (trombone), Gary Barnacle (sax) and Neil King (trumpet, uncredited on the sleeve) making up the Royal Guard Horns for the occasion. The B-side was 'Imperial Bedroom', a belated title track for the last album that had been intended for Frida of Abba who recorded her first solo release with Phil Collins as producer. Like its flip, though, it rather sounded as if it had been written round a title.

No, 1982 hadn't been a good year for singles – but Clive Langer's track record tended to suggest that if a producer's golden touch rubs off on the acts he works with then Costello's chart career was set to shine. Since providing the musical *hors d'oeuvres* on the 'Get Happy..' tour, Clive had enjoyed great singles success as producer with Madness, no fewer than nine consecutive releases making the UK Top Ten. And with Dexys Clive had tasted the ultimate – a platinum single for one million sales of 'Come On Eileen'. Not bad for a young man still in his twenties.

Langer and his co-producer Alan Winstanley were certainly an on-form studio combination. And after the artistic turmoil of the 'Imperial Bedroom' sessions, when Costello had produced himself, he naturally warmed to a man who had once declared, "We don't have any morals when it comes to studio craft. We always mix in sections, then stick it together afterwards."

The first fruits of the Langer/Winstanley/Costello collaboration arrived in February – and The Attractions were nowhere in sight. There was no cause for alarm, though, merely an invitation from Madness to contribute vocals to a slow, bluesier alternate take of 'Tomorrow's Just Another Day', a track from their 'Rise And Fall' album. The single of the band's original version of the song took a leaf out of Costello's book by including the jazzier interpretation as a bonus track on the flip of the 12-inch. As for the performance, Madness vocalist Graham 'Suggs' McPherson's comments underlined Costello's growing vocal prowess. "The original idea was to do a slow, bluesy version but I just couldn't get my tonsils round it…Elvis is really great, as good as I've ever heard him. Mind you, he *was* singing a good song for a change." And Elvis evidently agreed, since he guested on a couple of Madness dates in London and Brighton to lend them a hand with it.

After that unscheduled 'return' to Stiff Records courtesy of Madness, Elvis settled down to the more serious business of completing his first album with Langer and Winstanley. The producers had a reputation for clean, bright, uncluttered and commercial sounds if previous releases were anything to go by, and that promised a welcome relief from the claustrophobic and rather crowded ambience of 'Imperial Bedroom'. It remained to be seen how the horns would fit into the picture, since at least two of the new songs in the set at the Albert Hall gigs were performed either by Elvis solo ('The Comedians') or with keyboard accompaniment only ('Baby Pictures').

The chances of anybody outside the confines of the studio discovering the answer to these or any other questions, meanwhile, took a nosedive when it was learned that F-Beat's contract with Warners was up for renegotiation. Even if the bitter taste left by the dissolution of Radar Records was no longer fresh in Jake Riviera's mouth, it seemed unlikely that he'd re-sign on the dotted line without making the most thorough investigation of the alternatives. And so it proved; almost all the major labels spoke to Riviera in the coming months. It was to be high summer, August in fact, before 'Punch The Clock' was offered to a waiting world after a deal was concluded with the other Elvis' label, RCA Records, and their new managing director Dave Betteridge. This was the third time Costello's albums had been held up by business complications; Stiff kept 'My Aim Is True' two months in the warehouse while a distribution link was forged with Island, just as the Radar/F-Beat furore had later delayed 'Get Happy..'. But such experiences couldn't take the frustration out of delays.

Among the songs Costello slated for the album was one that, in its bitter cynicism, recalled the angrier moments of 'This Year's Model'. Far from being dated, however, 'Pills And Soap' was in its own fashion as contemporary as 'Shipbuilding', yet in a more oblique way. It started life as a piano backing track, played over the PA system as a suitably imposing overture to his Albert Hall performances. The lyrics, inspired by television news footage of a funeral in Northern Ireland, marvelled at the insensitivity of the media in covering such an event. Costello's train of thought ran to the manipulation of the "human animal, in all its many ways…particularly misplaced sentiment, including patriotism".

Down on Maggie's Farm, Britain was preparing itself for a

General Election, with Margaret Thatcher's ultra right-wing Conservative government predicted on course for a landslide victory. At least with 'Shipbuilding', Costello had been able to fire a shot across the bows; but with no distribution deal yet tied up, Costello's hands remained bound. Or did they? "It suddenly dawned on me," he said, "that there was nothing stopping me putting that record out on its own, as a single, under another name and on my own label." So it was that surprised music-paper editors found themselves receiving copies of 'Pills And Soap' by hand from the singer himself, and also the information that it would only be available until 9 June, Election Day, when it would be deleted. Costello's *nom de disque* would be taken from one of his 'Get Happy..' compositions: for a limited period only he would be The Imposter.

As it in fact transpired, 'Pills And Soap' was *not* deleted as intended, its appearance in the national charts having become too great a possibility for a hit-hungry Costello to ignore. And though it became his biggest self-penned single since 'Oliver's Army' when it reached number l6, ironically one week after the declaration of the expected Tory triumph, the episode was to many an unexpected climbdown by one of pop's most principled personalities – a feeling intensified when a near-identical 'remodelled version' was included on album.

Let this not detract, however, from the song's excellence. Even though its 150,000 purchasers failed to dent Thatcher's majority, it was clear that Costello's gift for political comment hadn't died with 'Night Rally'. And when it was revealed that Costello had cut his own version of 'Shipbuilding' for inclusion on the new album, one might have jumped to the conclusion that some kind of long-playing musical manifesto was in the offing – a supposition quickly dispelled by the next single, released one month prior to the album in July 1983. 'Everyday I Write The Book' ranks as one of Elvis' most catchy and commercial love songs. Written "in about half an hour in a hotel room in Derby" during The Attractions' last British tour, the song unveiled another unusual aspect of the new recording, namely the recruitment of Claudia Fontaine and Caron Wheeler, collectively Afrodisiak, to supply soulful backing vocals. This was Costello with a difference.

Indeed, so different was 'Punch The Clock' when it finally reached the shops in August that it took time to adjust to the presence of a four-man horn section and two additional singers, let alone the new production team. Yet if there were major changes in the studio sound and song arrangements, then the writing was still definitely and distinctively Costello.

The album started promisingly enough with the defiant Dexys-inspired riffing of 'Let Them All Talk', a track which (like the rest of the album) was better played loud. It was a song that seemed to have been written specifically for brass, and Elvis later confirmed that he had scored many of the songs himself. "The horn parts in some instances were my original writing. Then of course when the horn players themselves got hold of them their actual phrasing changed them slightly." Clive Langer, too, had "put in little punches" to help along what was "a real group effort".

The second side's opener, 'TKO (Boxing Day)' was very similar, a brassy, blustering number intended for dancing as much as listening – a policy to be commended, perhaps, in the lighter songs but rather less satisfactory when applied to 'The World And His Wife'. As Costello's demo of 'Girls Talk' had shown, his songs were strong enough to stand up to most styles and arrangements, even Linda Ronstadt's trilling or muzak. Yet the transformation from the thought-provoking acoustic ballad that opened the second Albert Hall gig to the version that made it on to vinyl was far from commendable. A 'fat' horn arrangement reminiscent of Brinsley Schwarz at their brassiest or, perish the thought, Boz Scaggs, successfully distracted and detracted from lyrics which, even by Costello's standards, had already been shoehorned into a far from roomy melody.

If the arrangements on 'Punch The Clock' were somewhat unusual for Elvis then there were still reference points aplenty for fans to navigate by. Two of the songs were, of course, more than familiar – 'Pills And Soap', remixed but not remodelled from its previous form, and his own version of 'Shipbuilding'. Now it's one thing writing a modern classic and another thing trying to better it – but whether or not Costello was wise to attempt a 'cover' (if indeed this qualified as one), he carried it off, thanks to a superbly under-stated vocal and the bonus of a breathtaking trumpet solo from American jazzman Chet Baker.

Costello's father and grandfather both played the trumpet, so he'd been a fan of the instrument long before he heard Baker's 'The Thrill Is Gone', a song that directly inspired the stunning ballad 'Almost Blue', written "with Chet Baker in mind" and recorded for 'Imperial Bedroom'. When the former Gerry Mulligan sideman, now in his fifties, came to the studio, The Attractions cut the backing track live in authentic jazz fashion, but their vocalist confes-sed to being rather overawed by the occasion. "I was the one who let the side down…I found it very difficult to sing live with him; although we got some of the vocal down I had to replace other parts of it." But the backing remained (and sounds) live, with string and organ overdubs added "to really bring out the real beauty of what he was playing."

The desirability of reproducing this on stage was one more reason why Elvis insisted on the TKO Horns adding a trumpet to their ranks, helping to forestall Dexys comparisons and "to give them a different sound…a warm, rich sound for some of the slower numbers." Session horn man Dave Plews was their choice, and his experience certainly added an extra element to the sound. Dave was also a member of Eurythmics' touring band, and although prior commitments led to his substitution on 'The World And His Wife' by Stuart Robson he returned to the fold for the upcoming tour.

If horns were an innovation, they couldn't obscure certain familiar phrases and feelings. Elsewhere we had flashbacks to former glories in 'The Greatest Thing', musically a cross between 'His Latest Flame' and 'Strict Time' and lyrically one of those rarities – a straight love song on an Elvis Costello album. Elvis described the song – a line from which named the album – as "a 1983 version of 'I Saw Her Standing There'." And was it just the clothing references in 'Everyday I Write The Book' that recalled the halcyon days of 'Alison'? That, and other little touches like the vocal quote from 'Accidents Will Happen' that opened 'Love Went Mad' gave a further tip of the hat to the past as Costello pursued his new musical direction.

Whatever its musical merits and demerits, 'Punch The Clock' wasn't going to go down in history as one of Elvis' most inspired albums in terms of his lyrics – wishing his listeners 'luck with a capital F' (in 'Love Gone Mad') and "making a silk purse from a sow's arse" ('Charm School') hardly put him in the running for the Laureate. But a song like 'Invisible Man', a nostalgic recollection of the cinema of his youth, had more than a touch of The Kinks' Ray Davies about it and, like 'New Amsterdam' on 'Get Happy..', provided an unexpected and welcome peep into the singer's fund of personal memories.

All in all the album showcased the most remarkable variety of musical styles since 'Trust' – from the Byrds-like harmonies of 'The Element Within Her' to the brass blast to 'TKO (Boxing Day)', contrasting the complex arrangement of the 'Imperial Bedroom' variety lavished on 'King Of Thieves' to one of his simplest ever in 'Pills And Soap'. And while Langer and Winstanley managed to keep the additional brass and vocal embellishments from muddying the overall sound (as was often to happen on the UK tour a few months later), the price to pay was a slightly flat, pat pop production that threatened to pull one or two of the musical punches.

With the album's release still eagerly awaited, Costello took the augmented Attractions on a series of low-publicity warm-up gigs prior to promoting 'Punch The Clock' in earnest. At least one of the TKO Horns, Jeff Blythe, was experiencing life on the road with Elvis for the first time – another ex-Dexys man, he'd replaced Brian Maurice in the line up just before the recording sessions, while Dave Plews was also making his live debut with them. Although

Afrodisiak weren't featured on either these or the American dates, they rejoined the set-up for the full British tour later in the year: these first gigs (Belfast and Dublin to make up for previous cancellations, a small number of college dates and a charity 'do' at Dingwalls) were 'strictly for the boys'.

If Elvis' stage manner had softened considerably in recent months, there were signs too that he was slowly but subtly changing his image. He'd adopted old-fashioned *pince-nez* glasses for the picture sleeve of 'Man Out Of Time', but the look he selected for 'Punch The Clock' with beret and large steel-framed spectacles all but took him back to the pre-Stiff days when he was still (a rather longer-haired) Declan McManus. And if he'd resisted the temptation to break the mould by actually smiling on an album cover, the fact that the picture was taken in Dublin before the warm-up gig there in June suggests that had the picture not been taken in soft focus, his Irish eyes just *might* have been.

By the time The Attractions plus guests reached the States in August, the eight-piece ensemble was red-hot. The routine never varied; the white-jacketed horn section would play at the beginning and end of the set, leaving the original quartet to play much of the older material alone. The split was about fifty-fifty, yet opinions were divided as to whether the horn arrangements on a few of the older songs were really necessary. They tended to blend well with the soul-influenced material from 'Get Happy..', yet the breathtaking dynamics of 'Clubland' and the drama of 'Watching The Detectives' could happily have shed the extra weight.

For all that, it was a brave experiment which had many observers drawing comparisons with Southside Johnny Lyon and occasionally even the soul revues of the Sixties; on the debit side, though, one reviewer cited Blood Sweat and Tears. Elvis had dug out some 'new' covers for the occasion, and most were American: Presley's 'His Latest Flame' (having tackled 'Little Sister', he now took on the B-side), Lee Dorsey's 'Working In A Coal Mine' and Laura Nyro's 'The Bells' were all added to the repertoire, along with The Easybeats' Sixties classic 'Friday On My Mind'. Off stage, meanwhile, it wasn't proving too difficult to find out what was on Elvis' mind – the man who once never gave interviews spoke to at least 50 different publications during the tour.

Costello kept some distinguished company in the States this time round. Tony Bennett invited him to perform a televised duet of 'It Don't Mean A Thing (If It Ain't Got That Swing)' – and since Elvis confessed that, "It was fun, although it's clear that he's a better singer than I am", it seemed that Count Basie's Orchestra held fewer fears after the nerves of the Albert Hall, 1982. Another of Costello's companions was Yoko Ono, who was compiling performances of her own songs by various artists. The cancellation of a gig in Louisiana gave The Attractions the opportunity to record 'Walking On Thin Ice' at Allen Toussiant's studio, an experience New Orleans music-lover Costello was unlikely to forget for a long time. The result was one of the more entertaining tracks on the album, 'Every Man Has A Woman', on which he and his band rubbed shoulders with Harry Nilsson, Roberta Flack and others and which was released nine months later.

As far as his own album went, the decision to concentrate once more on the American market boosted 'Punch The Clock' to number 24, and eventually a gold record for 500,000 sales, making this his most successful album there since 'Get Happy..'. Just as encouragingly, he broke his singles duck when 'Everyday' made it to number 36 – his first Hot Hundred forty-five. The tour also gave deserved exposure to Aztec Camera, a four-piece group from Scotland whose guitarist/songwriter Roddy Frame was held in the highest esteem by someone who had proved himself one of the best there is. "I wasn't that good when I was 19," Elvis said. "You won't be able to listen to him by the time he's 25 if he's that good now."

Costello clearly wasn't worrying too much about competition, though. His 'Clocking In Across The UK' tour simply picked up where the Stateside shows left off. With Afrodisiak now on board, there were ten people on the stage where once a single man had clutched his Jazzmaster – yet there was still no mistaking the central Attraction.

The choice of venues was restricted to dancehalls, a logical move considering the high-octane dance music served up. This had the side-effect of splitting the London dates into three points of the compass, South (Streatham Cat's Whiskers), North (Tottenham Mayfair) and West (Hammersmith Palais), on consecutive nights. As with the Albert Hall shows back in December/January, Elvis strolled on with acoustic guitar for a couple of numbers, or, alternatively, started with a keyboard-and-vocal rendition of 'Pills And Soap' before being joined by the rest of the band. More pointed political comment came in a post-election reprise of The Beat's 'Stand Down Margaret', the song which climaxed a powerful anti-Thatcher broadside in mid-set after 'Shipbuilding' and 'Big Sister's Clothes'. After all 1984, the year of Big Sister, was only a couple of short months away…

Singles-wise, 'Punch The Clock' fared exceptionally well compared with recent form. Both 'Pills And Soap' (number 16) and 'Everyday I Write The Book' (number 28) made the Top Thirty, while 'Shipbuilding' of course, charted in Robert Wyatt's version. Released in September to tie in with the tour, 'Let Them All Talk' failed to sustain the sequence of successes by only reaching number 59 but yielded another new track in 'The Flirting Kind' which was in contention for a place on the album right until the last moment. 'Everyday's' flipside, 'Heathen Town', was also a bonus, updating Gram Parsons with its lyrical allusions to 'sin city' and concluding mysteriously with some strange, unsettling mechanical laughter in the fade, while the 12-inch incorporated 'Night Time' from the 'beat revival' EP sessions.

If Elvis and his Attractions found the stage getting mighty crowded, as the song goes, then Steve Nieve for one was going to do something about it. Some nights would find him in Soho, London's very own 'Clubland', playing jazz piano at the L'Escargot restaurant behind one-time Animal Nightlife *chanteuse* Chrysta Jones. Not content with 50 per cent of the spotlight, he decided to go it alone: December saw his first official solo concert at the Duke of York Theatre in London's West End.

Some members of the audience might have wondered what they were letting themselves in for. The answer was a romp through Steve's newly-released solo album, 'Keyboard Jungle', which sneaked out quietly on Jake Riviera's Demon Records label that same month – but anyone who thought an evening of piano instrumentals would be boring had another think coming. Apart from introducing ex-Squeeze keyboardist Jools Holland to play a couple of boogie numbers, he encouraged participation by an audience that included Elvis and the remaining Attractions, and invited several astonished people up to play with him – pianists or not. Ten days later, though, he was back in his more accustomed side-stage position for three shows at Hammersmith Odeon on 21-22 December that finished the tour on a high note and gave Elvis the chance to dust off his gorilla suit once more.

So the year 1983 ended with Elvis Costello's commercial stock perhaps as high as it had been since the halcyon days of 'Armed Forces' and 'Get Happy..'. The chart performance of 'Punch The Clock' in reaching number 3, perhaps aided by the strongest single since 'Oliver's Army', certainly could not have been predicted with any confidence. At last, it seemed, Costello was adding to his hard core of faithful followers. Surprisingly, in view of his past style-switching from record to record, Elvis insisted in at least one interview that he would definitely be using the TKO Horns for the next album. And though the Langer/Winstanley production team had been guilty of producing what was in places a rather two-dimensional sound, their employment had done no harm at all in terms of sales. For someone who since 1977 had done his level best to remain outside fashion, Elvis Costello was becoming almost *too* popular...

Goodbye Cruel World?

As Elvis found back in 1977 with 'Saturday Night Live', rock and the visual media of television and cinema have never been the easiest of bedfellows. When cinema first 'picked up' rock in the mid Fifties as a selling point to attract a young audience, Bill Haley got a hit out of it but cinemas full of broken seats gave warning of a stormy union. After 'Blackboard Jungle' and 'Rock Around The Clock' came Elvis Presley, who ruffled the same feathers as his namesake some 20 years on – his crime was to move his body in a 'lewd and lascivious fashion'. From then onwards, with the odd exception (take a bow Jimi Hendrix and The Sex Pistols) the media was to keep rock firmly in its place.

It was no wonder, then, that a spontaneous performer like Costello hated video, television's ultimate teen panacea. Pre-packaged, sanitised and duly censored, this was the ultimate development of lip-synching – three minutes of perfectly predictable entertainment that was precisely one hundred and eighty seconds more than you'd find in the average Elvis Costello concert. In many ways music and television were further apart than ever in the mid Eighties – yet given the number of Costello songs that dealt with the media, from 'Less Than Zero' through 'Radio Radio', 'Green Shirt' and others, it might be considered surprising that Elvis hadn't attempted more television than just the odd video clip. His public image had softened with the passing years, and 1983 was to mark his first tentative steps screenwards.

Costello joined British Actors Equity in the summer, and his first screen role soon followed. Northern playwright Alan Bleasdale achieved great success with a one-off TV production, 'The Blackstuff', about an itinerant gang of roadbuilders and their adventures. His rough-hewn, intensely realistic characters translated well into a series, logically entitled 'Boys From The Blackstuff', focusing on each character in turn – indeed one in particular, Liverpudlian Yosser Hughes, became something of a folk hero, his catchphrase "gizza job" entering everyday use and even inspiring a couple of records. Such gifted characterisation invited comparison with Costello's own.

Bleasdale's next venture not only featured Elvis in a cameo role but boasted a brand-new song from his prolific pen. Building on the success of 'Yosser's Story' and likewise set in a Merseyside location, 'Scully' followed the schoolboy hero of the same name (played by Andrew Schofield) through various misadventures with friends, teachers, girls and – especially – football. Francis Scully's obsession with Liverpool Football Club echoed Costello's own youth. "I really liked football…I was fanatical about it," he says. "There was only one team for me." Inspired by the team's all-scarlet strip Costello wrote the show's theme 'Turning The Town Red', an acoustic guitar-based song with layered harmonies and one of his most beguiling melodies.

Most artists would have rush-released such a commerical tune with an appropriate picture sleeve to benefit from its weekly exposure – even if Britain's Channel 4 TV was still trying to shake off its minority interest tag. Criminally, 'Turning The Town Red' – a potential 'Oliver's Army' – was released only as the B-side of Costello's next single and will undeservedly become one of his lesser-known gems. As for the part in which Elvis made his acting debut on 21 May 1984, the role of Henry, Francis' retarded and railway-obsessed brother, was hardly a scene stealer – in fact it wasn't until the last episode of the series that he was given a speaking line. In his British Rail cap, headphones (through which he listened to loco recordings) and without the famous hornrims, it was easy to forget it was Elvis Costello on screen. Yet perhaps that revealed an art in itself…

Costello also made a brief appearance – as a 'stone deaf A&R man' – in 'The Bullshitters', a hilarious take off of the TV series 'The Professionals', which was screened on Channel 4 on November 3. Starring Keith Allen and Peter Richardson, The Bullshitters offered Elvis the opportunity to utter the immortal A&R man's line, "Let's do lunch, man". He received a smack in the teeth for his interest.

But for Elvis Costello, 1984 represented a blank canvas. If 'Armed Forces' ended his 'new wave' period and 'Punch The Clock' marked a return to form and popularity, then here was an opportunity to map out a new musical direction in the capable hands of his new producers, Messrs. Langer and Winstanley. As if to show he'd not lost the production touch himself, he helped out a friend in The Specials' Jerry Dammers, who spent so much time recording the band's third album that it eventually emerged with the title 'In The Studio'. By taking over, he lent what Dammers gratefully called "a fresh pair of ears" to 'Nelson Mandela', a glorious, barnstorming plea to free the jailed chairman of the African National Congress.

And when lead singer Stan Campbell quit on the day of a live 'Tube' TV broadcast Elvis happily lent his voice to the band too.

In global terms, the new year was welcomed with an Orwellian foreboding. In the UK, where the three million plus unemployment figure continued to rise, the welfare state and nationalised industries were battering down the hatches for the inevitable consequences of Margaret Thatcher's return to power. The long and bitter miners' strike that started in March was a clear sign that Big Sister was in implacable mood. Over in the United States the build-up to the presidential election campaign had already ground into motion, with all the signs that Ronald Reagan would emulate or even better Thatcher's landslide – and in terms of world peace, the consequences of *that* were too awesome to contemplate.

It was fitting, then, that Costello's first public proclamation of 1984 should see him once more adopt the Imposter pseudonym he'd used for 'Pills And Soap' to deliver another slice of mordant social comment. Premiered as a solo acoustic number at his Hammersmith Odeon show in December, 'Peace In Our Time' was in many ways the final instalment of a trilogy that began with 'Shipbuilding' and 'Pills And Soap'. Compared with the latter, its lyrics were unusually straightforward: "I don't think I have to explain the politics of the song this time," he remarked. "It's just a song I wanted out right now for reasons I think will be obvious when you hear it."

And so they were. The title, of course, evoked Chamberlain's worthless Munich Agreement of 1938 when the appeasement of Hitler made World War II a foregone conclusion. Costello turned the pages of his own history book with the British defence of the Falklands, the US invasion of Grenada and that same country's far from fictitious designs on outer space with the 'Star Wars' programme before indulging in a little crystal ball gazing concerning "a light over the sea burning brighter than the sun". In the nuclear age, surely no one could mistake the savage irony of his chorus "And we can thank God that we've finally got peace in our time."

Elvis frequently returned to the Sixties for inspiration, but never this way: 'Peace In Our Time' had all the hallmarks of an updated 'Eve Of Destruction'. This protest song of the Eighties, which he and The Attractions would be pleased to play at the Glastonbury CND Festival in June, was backed by a folk song from the previous decade, and one hardly less cheery at that. 'Withered And Died' was first released on Richard and Linda Thompson's 1973 LP 'I Want To See The Bright Lights Tonight'. Costello followed Thompson's career since his emergence as a leading light in late-Sixties folk-rock pioneers Fairport Convention, and he clearly found parallels to his own work in the singer/guitarist's darkly original world-view. Indeed, another Thompson song, 'End Of The Rainbow', was to enter Elvis' live repertoire during 1984, its chorus 'There's nothing at the end of the rainbow/There's nothing to grow up for anymore' reflecting the job prospects of so many school-leavers, especially in Costello's beloved Liverpool.

Richard Thompson's services were in demand for the recording of Costello's next album, slated for June release, but its typical three-week 'record-rehearse-mix' schedule found the guitarist in the United States and unable to participate. Prior to the record's appearance, Elvis also found time to visit the States in April for a three-week tour. Such ventures were nothing new, of course; indeed, his knowledge of the highways and byways (not to mention Holiday Inns) of North America was by now unrivalled. This time, though, it was to be just a single room – seven years after his triumphant solo sets at the Nashville in West Kensington to a crowd of barely 400, Elvis once more became a one-man band.

To an outsider, his preparations for the musical equivalent of exposing oneself in public were anything but methodical. "I still don't know what I'll be playing," he claimed the week before his departure, adding, "It's all a bit nerve racking really... (but) it'll be a change and a challenge which is the whole point of doing it."

And if the point needed to be proved, he did just that. Stepping briskly out of the side-stage shadows, he picked up his acoustic guitar and strummed confidently into the first selection of numbers old, not so old and not yet revealed. Some songs were transformed by the absence of their previously elaborate arrangements ('Green Shirt', 'Kid About It' and a very slow 'Riot Act' in particular), while others might have been made for it (Stranger In The House').

Without an electric backing to overcome this time, Costello's vocals were particularly confident, leading him to give old favourites new twists; the impassioned interpolation of Joe Tex's 'The Love You Save Might Be Your Own' in 'Alison' was as sacred as it was sacrilegious. 'Peace In Our Time' drew impassioned cheers as Costello sang the lines "There's already one spaceman in the White House/What d'you want another one for?" (referring to candidates Ronald Reagan and ex-astronaut John Glenn), just as post-Nixon America cheered Dylan to the echo ten years previously when he pointed out that "Even the President of the United States has sometimes got to stand naked." As if to underline the comparison, the ever-iconoclastic Elvis even dared to include a Dylan song ('I Threw It All Away' from 'Nashville Skyline') among the encores.

The tour attracted praise from all quarters, most critics commenting on the new-found audibility of his lyrics and his top-notch vocal form. Most concerts lasted around one and a half to two hours with a good deal of banter between songs. The entertainment value was heightened by an appropriate choice of support – T-Bone Burnett, a lanky, ungainly singer-songwriter from Texas soon to sign for Jake Riviera's Demon label. The two transatlantic troubadours complemented each other perfectly – and this was not to be the last time they shared a stage.

As Costello headed westwards across the Pacific to join The Attractions for an Australasian tour, the new album was announced. 'Goodbye Cruel World' was its title, the cover photograph showing Steve Nieve in fencing gear atop a cliff in the South of France with the other three band members standing round. The source of its originally intended title – 'Pat And Mike', a painting by Eamonn Singer – adorned the inner sleeve. Recorded at SARM West Studios, London, and supervised by the Langer/Winstanley team that had played such efficient midwives to 'Punch The Clock', Elvis' album provided balm where its predecessor had offered bluster – and nowhere was this more apparent than its first single, 'I Wanna Be Loved'. The very idea of the Elvis Costello of old crooning this ballad released on Imperial in 1959 by teen idol Ricky Nelson and later revived by Teachers Edition would have been enough to make any self-respecting fan choke – but if this was easy listening, it was admittedly pop music with class.

With the exception of the Nashville sessions with Billy Sherrill where Costello half-heartedly subjected himself to the rigid artist/producer relationship that typified country music since it began, Elvis had never encountered a producer whose ideas differed so radically from his own. And whereas Nick Lowe's task in years past had been to coax the best possible sound from Jake Riviera's *enfant terrible* in the confines of the recording studio with the least trouble, the interaction between Langer, Winstanley and Costello was clearly somewhat more creative. That's not to decry 'Basher' Lowe's straightforward production methods – the aural sensations of 'Imperial Bedroom' attest to the initial consequences of his absence – but while 'Punch The Clock' found the new producers filling the breach, they were clearly now calling some of the shots.

The song that most perfectly illustrates the process is undoubtedly 'The Only Flame In Town', which started life as an agonised, heartfelt ballad in Elvis' solo repertoire – a lovestruck lover protesting his independence. As the composer himself noted, it was "like a straightforward classic R&B ballad…(until) Clive persuaded me to get a slightly more interesting rhythm going". The result was a high-gloss chunk of what the Americans call AOR – adult oriented rock – in 6/8 time. And who better to help out with the high harmonies than the crown prince of AOR himself, Daryl Hall? "I can get up to the harmony," claimed Costello, "but it would sound quite harsh…and also I get a bit tired of hearing my own voice harmonising with myself." A visit backstage at a Hall and Oates Wembley gig that March clinched the deal.

Hall's harmony vocal took only an hour to record – a tribute indeed to his professionalism. And, though Elvis professed himself "not a major fan" of Hall and Oates, he swallowed his reservations to perform with Hall in a rather cheesy video for the single, shot in Australia, which saw them serenading two young ladies at a restaurant table. One way and another, this was about as far from the public image of Elvis Costello as he'd ever gone – the man who once proclaimed he'd "rather go back to Liverpool" than chase success in the US seemed to be embracing said notion with both arms. Sadly, the gesture was not to be reciprocated: although Daryl Hall was to enjoy three tastes of the US Top Ten in 1984 (including a number 1 hit), these were obtained with his more usual crooning companion John Oates; with 'Only Flame' progressing no further than number 56, it's perhaps unsurprising he decided not to change a winning team.

Most of the songs on 'Goodbye Cruel World' were born in an office at F-Beat's West London headquarters in Acton where Elvis locked himself away in January and February to concentrate on writing after some criticism of the content of his previous long-player. "A burst of songwriting like that," he claimed later, "can sometimes get a sort of tension into it that perhaps was lacking in some of the lesser songs on the last album." To the fruits of his early-year labours were added 'I Wanna Be Loved', 'Inch By Inch' – previously entitled 'Goody Two Shoes' but rewritten in the wake of the Adam Ant hit – and 'The Great Unknown', a number debuted on the 'dancehall' tour of 1983 and co-written with producer Langer. Strangely, although Costello has publicly acknowledged his collaborator before and since, the song is credited on the album to Costello alone. 'The Comedians' finally made an appearance on record, having been one of Elvis' solo entry numbers at the Albert Hall in Christmas 1982-83 but it returned to the guitar case shortly afterwards until its reappearance here.

As with his previous 'incognito' protest songs, Elvis chose to include a version of his Imposter release, making the album's thirteenth and final track. A reason for Costello's decision was probably the fact that this would provide exposure for the song in the US where, due to its British release on the IMP label, it hadn't yet appeared. Strangely enough, it was its predecessor on side two, the uptemp 'Deportees Club', that ran into trouble in the States; during a live radio broadcast in Philadelphia the line "In America the Law is a piece of ass" was excised from the transmission by an alert censor. The meaning of the song is difficult to follow without the aid of the inner-sleeve lyric sheet, so one can only assume that the arbiter in question had done his homework.

Just as 'The Greatest Thing' from the previous album owed its ancestry to a stage cover version the first few notes of 'Sour Milk Cow Blues' sounded suspiciously like the intro to 'Working In A Coal Mine'; Costello even came to introduce it as such on stage in the 1984 UK tour. But any similarity was, as they say in the movies, coincidental; once unleashed, the song's feel and tempo quickly changed. Aside from the instrumental nod to Lee Dorsey, the title had been 'borrowed', too; the original 'Milk Cow Blues' written by bluesman Sleepy John Estes, was recorded by the other Elvis – Presley, that is – in his Sun Records period. With two steals in one song, Elvis must have been taking tips from Nick Lowe…

Shorn of the horn arrangements that lent such warmth to its long-playing predecessor, 'Goodbye Cruel World' would automatically have seemed a more melancholy affair by comparison. As it was, a chill vein of realism ran through the choice of material, even the older songs like 'The Comedians' and 'The Great Unknown' slotting perfectly into the prevailing mood as if written specifically for the purpose. The most personal song of the set had to be 'Home Truth'. Following hard on the heels of 'The Only Flame In Town', it took that song's protestations with the story of a relationship grown cold to their heartbreaking conclusion. Rumours that the song all too closely mirrored Elvis' own domestic situation were given credence by his admission that "Clive Langer advised me to keep 'Home Truth' off the album. He said keep those things to yourself, that's better. But I'm not the only person in the world who's watched his relationship go downhill."

As if to symbolise this slip into depression, the lyrics of 'Joe Porterhouse' shared the same tune as an earlier song, 'I Love You When You Sleep', the gentle words of a lover now replaced by the story of a strong man brought to his knees. Even the album's obligatory tilt at the media, 'Worthless Thing', was couched in a personal vein. It wasn't until the last verse when Costello suggested taking a cable and "sticking it down your throat" that the meaning became clear – it wasn't some witless woman he was talking about but that faithless tramp MTV, the all-music cable channel whose patronage makes or breaks artists in the US as much on their fashion sense as their music. Ironically, though he might not be 'ten feet taller and almost handsome', Costello might have saved a lot of time, trouble and touring bills had MTV been around to spread his image in the late Seventies, yet the concept of so much power in so few hands was one he was never going to buy. His stage introduction to 'Worthless Thing' said it all: "About 30 years ago, there was a kind of music that was very popular with people who put lots of grease in their hair. Nowadays, we have wires that come into our living rooms and bring this music into our homes."

Live, then, it was clear that Elvis was as acerbic as ever. And on record, it seemed Langer and Winstanley had brought home the bacon. Despite several differences of opinion between producers and artist – Costello demanded the drums be turned up on 'Room With No Number', for instance, because he "figured there was the danger of it becoming too sweet" – the result was a mature and listenable album with none of the over-indulgence that had marred 'Imperial Bedroom'. If the two singles (neither of which charted in the UK) were the slickest of Costello's confections, then the writing, arrangement and performance of a song like 'Home Truth' could stand with his best. And, as with the great majority of his work, 'Goodbye Cruel World' fully repaid further listenings, proving that Costello's talents remained active under this new-found commercial gloss.

As the dust settled on Elvis' annual record release, The Attractions slipped into gear for the customary spot of roadwork, once more concentrating on the States in preference to the many and various delights of Olde England, where the album reached number 10 but stayed only two weeks in the Top Twenty. Given the scale of his US touring in 1984, both solo and with The Attractions, it was surprising that 'Goodbye Cruel World' halted its promising rise through *Billboard's* album chart at number 35, but this failed to take the shine off what was generally regarded as one of his better tours. A family atmosphere was assured by the presence of Nick Lowe, Martin Belmont, Paul Carrack and the rest of the first-named's new Cowboy Outfit who opened the shows. In Austin, Texas, Elvis and The Attractions repaid the compliment with a surprise guest appearance on one of Lowe's solo gigs, pulling a couple of 'new oldies' out of the hat in Wilson Pickett's 'Midnight Hour' and Larry Williams' 'Slow Down', the latter a 'rediscovered' cover from the 'Get Happy..' sessions. Elvis and Nick also performed a quavering version of 'Baby It's You', the old Shirelles' hit covered by The Beatles on their début album. Their record of the song achieved notoriety by turning up as a bonus track on 12-inchers by *both* artists on either side of the Atlantic. If ever a gig was itself a collectors' item, then that particular date must surely qualify for the accolade.

Elsewhere, the band turned in torrid, high-energy sets of up to 34 songs, ranging throughout the Elvis repertoire yet with a greater bias towards 'current product' than in past years. The two songs to receive barely an airing from 'Cruel World' were 'Joe Porterhouse', perhaps the least durable of the album's tracks, and 'Room With No Number' – the latter being one of its most arranged tracks with multi-dubbed keyboards. As previously mentioned, Costello admitted that the track as recorded differed radically from his conception of the song. Combined with the fact that 'The Only Flame In Town' was being played at some gigs in two forms – the sweetened upbeat (currently available) version and the anguished ballad original – the omission of 'Room With No Number' suggested that Costello was beginning to regard his recorded and live work as two very separate entities.

January 1984 saw Jake's former partner Dave Robinson merge Stiff with a larger independent, Chris Blackwell's Island Records. Though F-Beat maintained its freedom of movement, it now walked hand in hand with RCA – and past events had taught Riviera not to put all his eggs in one basket. By assigning Costello's back catalogue (with the exception of 'My Aim Is True' which stayed with Stiff), to the IMP label, he ensured the records' continued availability regardless of the vagaries of fashion and economics. Elvis' own label released its first single by another artist late in 1983: 'The Captain And The Kings', a quirky Brendan Behan song from the play 'The Hostage', was produced by Colin Fairley and the Imposter and sung by former Radiators From Space leader Philip Chevron. This was joined in 1984 by the debut release from 'punkabilly skiffle' combo The Men They Couldn't Hang. Though he self-mockingly proclaimed he was "joining the ranks of the Paul Wellers with my own record label", Elvis was more interested in one-off projects than actively seeking new talent. "If a lot of things turn up, then I'll release a lot of good records," he said – and with the lion's share of his back catalogue under lock and key, he'd not made a bad start.

Autumn found Costello finally homeward bound, bringing in tow sax-player Gary Barnacle who appeared with him on the album and some of the Stateside dates. Recognising that some 'Punch The Clock' material might lose out with the absence of 1983's soul revue line-up of horns and backing singers, Elvis enlisted Barnacle's aid to add his slick sax lines to selected songs. In a curious echo of his father's career, in which Hammersmith Palais became a second home, he chose to play a residency at the West London dancehall, performing every Monday in October to packed houses and touring in the week. That wasn't all it echoed, either – it was nearly seven years to the month that Costello and The Attractions packed out the Nashville in the residency that had stoked the fires of legend. In October 1984, Elvis Costello *was* the only flame in London town.

It was, perhaps, his greatest showcase since the ill-fated Dominion gigs of 1979 – but the lessons had been learned. Touring in the States gave home audiences the chance to get used to the album before it was served up live – and while this made the repast a little predictable in comparison with the feasts of yesteryear, there was still plenty of meat. The venue was perfect, the audiences willing and able to bop 'til they dropped. And that was literally what happened, with sets extending almost until the chimes of midnight and rendering one of the encore numbers, 'I Can't Stand Up For Falling Down', prophetically true. Not that anyone was *too* worried…

In many ways, these shows were a return to the full-tilt performances of 1978, even country covers like Johnny Cash's 'I Still Miss Someone' and the Burritos' 'Dark End Of The Street' were given little chance to linger in the memory. But if the set itself showed one side of Costello, the four solo encores – 'End Of The Rainbow', 'Riot Act', 'High Fidelity' and a stunning version of 'The Image Of Me' written by Harlan ('The Streets Of Baltimore') Howard – were nothing short of breathtaking. And this cherry on the cake was something to whet the appetite for Elvis' recently-announced solo tour, a repeat of his Stateside adventure with T-Bone Burnett once more taking care of the warm-up chores. "He just called me up and asked me to open for him on his tour," commented the affable American. "I guess he wanted some meat to throw on stage before he came on."

Given the success of Rockpile's 'Girls Talk' cover, it was perhaps surprising that Costello compositions hadn't provided chart material for more discerning artists over the years. Yet if one ignores Ronstadt's passing infatuation, few dared essay their own interpretations of what was, in the main, a body of intensely per-sonal songs. In 'Girl's Talk's ' case, of course, Elvis' own demo didn't surface until Dave Edmunds' version was widely known as the 'original' – yet the fact that a good percentage of the people who made it a hit single couldn't have known (or possibly cared) of its authorship attested to the possibilities there. Rumour had it that Mari Wilson and Robert Plant – as different performers as one could imagine – requested material for forthcoming album projects, while Elvis confirmed that he was writing for Alison Moyet, the bluesy ex-vocalist of Yazoo now starting a solo career and a young Scottish group called Sunset Gun. He'd met Alison (Alf to her friends) on BBC Radio 1's Round Table in June 1982 and kept in touch, but her excellent debut LP released in mid 1984 included a song from Motown's Lamont Dozier but none from Costello.

It seemed more than possible that with the passage of time Elvis might concentrate less on recording and touring and more on becoming a songwriter in the Broadway tradition he admired so much. Besides, with his own output now averaging an annual album, there was plainly inspiration to spare, and 1984 saw Elvis chance his arm once more in the made-to-measure songwriting stakes. First to benefit was Tracie, teenage protégée of former Jam frontman Paul Weller, who was attempting to start a 'British Soul' label in his Respond operation. Costello and Weller, arguably

British rock's two most politically conscious performers, met and made friends at an anti-Cruise missile charity show, 'The Big One', staged in London on 18 December 1983. The result of Weller's request for new material for Tracie was 'I Love You When You Sleep', a haunting ballad acclaimed as the best track on the singer's debut album and duly released as a single in May. The song's tune, a close relation to 'Accidents Will Happen', was particularly memorable – so much so that Elvis re-used the melody for 'Joe Porterhouse', another set of lyrics on his own album.

The second grateful recipient had already helped Dave Edmunds and Nick Lowe turn 'Girls Talk' into a hit – Rockpile's former lead guitarist Billy Bremner. Sadly he failed to repeat the performance with 'Shatterproof', even though the radio exposure it gleaned made it, in the words of the singer, one of "Britain's most played non-hits." Some reviews were less than enthusiastic – *No. 1's* Max Bell minted a brand new rock cliche with the phrase "musical Polyfilla" – but whether or not Elvis rated this tale of domestic discord narrated in the third person as one of his lesser efforts we can but guess. At any rate, it wasn't to grace its author's own stage repertoire that year.

The omission of such songs as 'Shatterproof', 'Turning The Town Red' and 'Hoover Factory' was perhaps the major disappointment of Costello's solo UK shows. His repertoire spread the net fairly wide – 'This Year's Model' and 'Armed Forces' were the only albums not represented – but didn't dig quite deep enough into the songs his fans would most have liked to hear.

That said, the 'house full' signs up and down the country attested to the fact that, for many people, Elvis Costello baring his soul with a mere acoustic guitar for cover was always going to be the rock event of the year. His cheek in booking London's Royal Festival Hall – an acoustical dream compared with most rock venues and a haunt of classical music buffs – was rewarded when all 2,909 tickets sold out on the day they went on sale. Another factor behind the sudden sellout could well have been the growing feeling that Costello was planning some sort of major decision on his future. At the Dominion in November, where he'd returned after five years to play a rare 'sit-down' concert to conclude The Attractions' London dates, he announced that "This is the last concert that we'll be playing for a very, very, very long time…" The stage was set for surprises.

He strode on to the curiously empty Festival Hall podium and, without pausing to tune up, strummed straight into an acoustic 'Girls Talk', ending on the plea 'Can't you talk any louder?" repeated half-a-dozen times for effect. Talking was something he seemed quite happy to do. "This is the end of the year for me – it's my New Year's Eve," he confided to a hushed, attentive audience.

Switching from acoustic guitar to a Telecaster electric and back again, he could take it as read he was among friends, announcing only one song. "Man Called Uncle," he claimed, reminded him of the venue whose hoarding was alphabetically lacking. "They didn't have enough letters to spell my name," he said, "so they just put 'Elvis solo'…"

If the repertoire included few rarities from the past, Elvis clearly felt that his solo treatment of previously recorded material was interesting enough to demand attention – and with hungry young performers like Billy Bragg contesting the critical vote, there was a good deal of pride at stake here. 'Only Flame' was perhaps predictably performed in its original ballad form – and was all the better for it – while the treatment of the mass of his back catalogue that lay between those two selections varied from a 'Big Yellow Taxi' – like romp through 'Red Shoes' to a slow, stunning 'World And His Wife', now back in its original Albert Hall format.

The selections from 'Imperial Bedroom' gained immeasurably by being shorn of all studio trickery and ornamentation, while the 'Get Happy..' songs tended to sound more perfunctory and two-dimensional outside of a band setting. The honourable exception to the latter rule was a downtempo 'High Fidelity' which resurfaced as a solo encore in his recent UK shoes, took on a minor-key tinge and with it a new poignancy. The two Imposter releases or 'protest' songs seemed more than at home in the context of solo performance, the key line of 'Peace In Our Time' now reading petulantly 'What do you want the same one *again* for?'

The youthful enthusiasm that suffused his vocal-and-guitar excursions must have taken him back to his days as D.P. Costello, playing at folk clubs for little more than a pie and a pint. Something he'd never done then – and indeed seemed much more nervous about now – was play keyboards: but the Festival Hall, rather larger than the average folk club, offered a grand piano as well as the Wurlitzer electric parked next to the spare guitar. He took to the grand for a studied rendition of 'Almost Blue', and followed it with an instrumental piece cryptically identified as being "for a film that hasn't been made yet". Hunched over the more familiar and less imposing Wurlitzer, he coaxed the utmost from his limited technique with renditions of 'Shipbuilding' and a revamped 'Motel Matches' from 'Get Happy..'

As with his band concerts a couple of months previously, Costello was unstinting in his performance, playing well over two dozen songs. The set was enjoyably extended by the return of T-Bone Burnett, who'd once more been allotted the warm-up chores, to make up the 'Coward Brothers' and give Elvis a chance to wheel out a selection of golden and not-so-golden oldies. Johnny Cash's 'She Thinks I Still Care', The Beatles' 'Baby's In Black' (a country song John Lennon might have been surprised to find he'd written) and Scott McKenzie's fabled 'San Francisco' were all treated with the same mock reverence, and each ended with large stereo smiles. Costello looked as if he was having *fun* dammit. The experience was clearly something Burnett, for one, hadn't yet tired of: "We'll probably do another tour when the money runs out," he joked afterwards. But would there ever *be* another tour? As the last acoustic guitar chord died, Costello, dressed in buttoned black shirt, black trousers and plum crushed velvet jacket, gravely delivered his parting shot – "You won't see me for a long time."

Curiously, none of the music papers picked up on the significance of events – it was almost as if there were a conspiracy of silence. Elsewhere, he introduced 'I Hope You're Happy Now' as "the next single"; together with his valedictory message, it all added up to a bleak outlook for Costello fans. Rumours began to surface – he was going to live in New York, he'd quit The Attractions, he was to revert to his real name, he was producing an album by his tour support act, The Pogues – but no official word surfaced. All of a sudden it seemed highly appropriate that the last word from Costello on vinyl, appearing on a charity long-player, 'Sometimes A Great Notion', in November, was the fourth of the 'beat revival' EP tracks to surface – The Merseybeats' 'Really Mystified'. Could this *really* be goodbye, cruel world?

Only A Northern Folksinger

"How are yer? I want you to help me sing this old Northern English folksong." With this laconic greeting a bearded Elvis Costello strummed his way into the opening bars of 'All You Need Is Love' and back into the limelight he'd threatened to quit forever not six months previously.

His July appearance at Wembley Stadium as part of Live Aid, Bob Geldof's intercontinental fund-raising extravaganza for Ethiopia, wasn't just a contrast to his previous dark hints about retirement. It was short, succinct and to the point, promoting nothing but a message for the day. And, curiously enough, appearing in front of over a billion TV viewers continued Costello's 1985 ploy of letting lots of people see little bits of him.

The Attractions reconvened in March for another benefit concert, this one for the miners' strike which had, ironically, collapsed in disarray only days before. The crowd, at London's Logan Hall, saw Billy Bragg turn in a powerful solo set, yet had to wait a while as Costello and The Attractions took time to rekindle their partnership. There were new songs among the old favourites – but these were destined to remain mere titles for those who weren't fortunate enough to be there. For a matter of weeks later Elvis Costello confounded expectations once more by releasing a 'Best Of' album.

To say the release was unexpected is no exaggeration. And the manner in which it was marketed was no less surprising: this was a TV-promoted disc on the Telstar label, dressed in a totally unbecoming cover (an artist's illustration that better resembled Sir Robin Day) and devoid of the explanatory sleeve notes that had made '10 Bloody Marys' such a joy. In short, it seemed thrown together – and several months too late for the Christmas market at that.

It was difficult, though, to quibble with the 18-track selection. All the chart singles were present and correct (with the exception of the acerbic 'Radio Radio'), and these were spiced up with a handful of more famous album tracks, notably 'Shipbuilding' and the critically acclaimed 'New Lace Sleeves' from 'Trust'. Each of Costello's nine studio albums were represented to a greater or lesser degree, and the excellence of the music persuaded sufficient numbers of record-buyers to look past the 'son of *Smash Hits*' cover art and propel 'The Best Of Elvis Costello – The Man' to number 8 in May.

Unbeknown to many of his fans, Elvis had another stake in the May 1985 album charts as a contributor to Eurythmics' new album, 'Be Yourself Tonight'. At first glance it was a ridiculous pairing in more ways than one – the brittle, electropop duo with Elvis' openly emotional approach, not to mention the statuesque Annie Lennox with her diminutive new partner. Yet as if to confound such irreverent preconceptions, the vocal pairing on 'Adrian' worked amazingly well, leaving Costello far from overawed by fellow 'guest stars' Stevie Wonder and Aretha Franklin who also appeared on the album. Interestingly, too, it was Costello's first recorded duet with a female vocalist: one hoped from this evidence that it wouldn't be the last.

With the success of his own album (strangely enough without too much TV advertising in the initial stages), two of the lesser known tracks suddenly found themselves on either side of a single. Concealed on the flip was 'Beyond Belief', 'Imperial Bedroom's sole contribution to the long-playing venture, while the A-side aired 'Green Shirt'. There is no denying that the synthetic bubble 'n' squeak of the 'Armed Forces' cut had worn well and justified its single exposure. Yet the corny advertising slogan 'Number 1 in a series of 2', green vinyl and a 12-inch remix by Colin Fairley smacked of ersatz ZTT. Where Jake Riviera had once led with his witty sloganeering, this seemed a half-hearted imitation of his rivals.

From Elvis' point of view, such gimmicks were unnecessary, and he voiced his disapproval of "peace sign picture discs like the kind of crap they're doing now with 'Green Shirt'. It just devalues the song." The remark suggested that RCA, having been denied the opportunity of releasing the album, had tried rather too hard to capitalise on the single. Earlier that year ex-label boss turned pop pundit Jonathan King had remarked on RCA's ability to 'lose' such quality singles as Hall and Oates' 'Out Of Touch', a US number 1 in 1984 that failed to make the UK Top 40. If the label was out to prove a point to Riviera and Costello with their marketing of 'Green Shirt' a final chart placing of number 68 tells its own story. Yet with just two Top 30 entries since 1981, did anyone really expect otherwise?

A reminder of the glorious days when Elvis *did* have hit singles came with the video complement to the album release. Also titled 'The Best Of Elvis Costello – The Man', it collected all his promotional clips from 1978's 'Pump It Up' to 'The Only Flame In Town' six years later. Ironically, much of the contents would have been more familiar to viewers of MTV in the States than fans in his native land – yet it was a joy to re-view the adventurous graphics of 'Accidents Will Happen' courtesy of Rocky Morton and Annabel Jankel, the duo who have since created 'Max Headroom'. In contrast to such authentic pop history 'Watching The Detectives', for which no video existed (how times have changed since 1977…), now had a video spliced together from old detective movie footage. All in all, the tape made essential viewing amid the year's usual glut of regurgitated pop promos and half-baked concepts.

Elvis appeared in the flesh too, and rather more often these days; in fact he seemed to be playing anywhere and with anyone who'd have him. An early year solo set prior to The Pogues' headliner at the Hammersmith Clarendon and an encore appearance with longtime friend John Hiatt at the Duke of York's Theatre in April both added to his surprisingly high profile – and that was more than welcome in what was shaping up to be one of Eighties pop's most tedious years.

He'd clearly benefited from the rest, confiding to *NME's* Mat Snow that "It'd been seven years without any longer than a month's break and two years with five days' holiday." Explaining his pessimistic remarks of the previous year, he revealed that he'd been "getting bored… I was working on complete nervous energy for the last couple of months."

He duetted with Hiatt on the American's 'Warming Up To The Ice Age' album, providing the harmony voice on a reading of The Detroit Spinners' soul oldie 'Living A Little Laughing A Little' and it was this he recreated on stage: the track was later released as a single. The Pogues' connection was both professional and personal: he was not only fulfilling the role of producer on their 'Rum, Sodomy And The Lash' LP, a Top 20 entry later in '85, but was also seen about with the group's female bass player Caitlin O'Riordan; enquiries by *The Sun* as to the nature of this relationship were greeted with tirades of abuse such as hadn't been heard since '78. Some things, it seemed, never changed…

The IMP label was going great guns, too. Though The Pogues had been snared by Dave Robinson at Stiff, Costello still had The Men They Couldn't Hang. This Southampton quintet's sensitive interpretation of Eric Bogle's folky 'Green Fields Of France' dominated the indie charts for fully six months before their 'Ironmasters' LP, produced by Elvis' lieutenant Phil Chevron, drew further acclaim. Wearing his label-bosses hat for a rare interview, Costello memorably summed up IMP as being "like a photocopier or an inflatable doll – you just get it out when you need it."

A curious addition to the IMP roster was Agnes Bernelle, a Dublin-based Berliner whose cabaret-style interpretations of the poems of Joachim Ringelnatz ("the German Edward Lear") set to music became the label's very first LP, 'Father's Lying Dead On The Ironing Board'. And Agnes' curiosity value (akin to Stiff's signing of Max Wall back in the good old days) led to nationwide exposure on Terry Wogan's BBC-TV chat show. A genial Costello, roped in to appear, seemed somewhat embarrassed to be receiving the lion's share of Wogan's attention: a remark to the effect that he was Declan McManus, *not* Elvis Costello, set tongues wagging in a repeat of the 'reversion to real name' story, but nothing much more came of it.

No, 1985 needed Elvis Costello as much as ever, regardless of what he wished to call himself. With Billy Bragg making a spirited challenge for the Imposter's crown, Graham Parker making yet another comeback with yet another label and Paul Weller still pouring his talent down the drain as a blue-eyed soul rebel, there was clearly still room for a talent of this magnitude. Yet there were signs of a rethink in recording terms when Elvis revealed that he considered 'Goodbye Cruel World' to be "the worst record of the best songs that I've written". Similar comments after the commercial failure of 'Trust' preceded the split with Nick Lowe – so it wasn't surprising that August found him ensconced in the studio with T-Bone Burnett behind the mixing desk.

This wasn't the first Coward Brothers reunion since the Festival Hall: Elvis' only all-new record release of the year so far was in July when The Cowards put their names to 'The People's Limousine' on IMP. Issued with no perceptible advertising, the single got the unlikely-looking Brothers the cover of *Melody Maker* but precious few radio plays. An appearance at London's Duke of York's Theatre preceded their flight to Los Angeles, where The Attractions joined them a few days later.

While their leader was disporting himself on stage, screen and gossip column, The Attractions found diverse ways of occupying their time. Steve Nieve was undoubtedly keeping the most exalted company, lending his talents to Mick Jagger and David Bowie's chart-topping cover of 'Dancing In The Street' recorded for Live Aid and produced in the States by the Langer-Winstanley partnership. Steve also played on albums by Madness and The Damned. Pete Thomas, meanwhile, chose to rediscover the London pub circuit, playing with Big Heat, a band featuring ex-Inmate Bill Hurley and ex-Key Drew Barfield whose cracking debut single, 'Watch Me Catch Fire', was produced by Elvis and ignored by the public. Pete's final workout before jumping the Jumbo was a short UK tour with his former boss John Stewart – and, as usual, the entrance fee to Stewart's low-key dates was worth it for Thomas' contribution alone.

The question of why The Attractions didn't appear at Live Aid still remained unanswered – and Bruce Thomas, for one, was said to have queried his leader's decision to appear alone. But his arrival in the States with his fellow Attractions forestalled any split rumours.

Fifteen of the songs that were likely to make up the album had already been previewed when Costello played a secret club gig (as 'The Pope Of Pop') at London's Portlands in late April. Titles like 'The Big Light', 'Brilliant Mistake', 'We Don't Even Try Anymore' and 'Poisoned Road' were country-flavoured and delivered with minimal guitar accompaniment and maximum vocal passion.

Given the fact that at least one of the songs had been co-written with bass guitarist John Doe of LA punks X (who, revealingly, had just started a country-rock spinoff group with Dave Alvin of The Blasters) and T-Bone Burnett had produced Los Lobos' acclaimed 'How Will The Wolf Survive' for the Slash label, all the omens suggested that the critically heralded wave of US guitar music would exert an influence on the recording. As far as Costello was concerned, he could name "half a dozen bands in America that I think are really great which I can't in England. So that means to me that American music is more interesting at the moment."

If an advance taster of Elvis' songwriting form in September was any guide, the muse was certainly working overtime. He gave Nick Lowe his second-ever Costello composition (after 'Girls Talk') to cover on his album 'The Rose Of England'. 'Indoor Fireworks' was the title, the song itself a real slow-burning cracker. Its closest relations were 'Motel Matches' (both in tempo and its incendiary metaphors) and Billy Bremner's 'Shatterproof': the story of "sparks behind closed doors" that led to the writer building "a bonfire of my dreams" hinted at real-life heartache and inspired an unusually emotional vocal from Lowe aided by an uncredited back-up harmony from EC himself. If Costello had songs *this* good to give away, there were clearly more treats in store…

At 2.06pm on 13 July 1985 Elvis Costello took his leave of the Wembley stage. The afternoon's entertainment was strictly musical – and, if previous few in the worldwide audience fully appreciated Elvis' choice of song for the occasion, that was too bad. 'All You Need Is Love' had, after all, been the song The Beatles recorded for 'Our World', the first ever round-the-world satellite TV link-up in June 1967. So it was with a tip of the hat to the past that Costello strode off stage and into his future. To the relief of his many followers, he'd changed his tune – not so much 'Goodbye Cruel World' now as 'Abide With Me'. The fans might be on the pitch but the game, it seemed, was still far from over.

Discography

UK Releases

Singles

Less Than Zero/Radio Sweetheart	March 77	Stiff BUY 11
Alison/Welcome To The Working Week	May 77	Stiff BUY 14
Red Shoes/Mystery Dance	July 77	Stiff BUY 15
Watching The Detective/Blame It On Cain (Live): Mystery Dance (Live)	October 77	Stiff BUY 20
(I Don't Want To Go To) Chelsea/You Belong To Me	March 78	Radar ADA 3
Stranger In The House/Neat Neat Neat (Live) (Bonus with 'This Year's Model' LP)	March 78	Radar SAM 83
Pump It Up/Big Tears	June 78	Radar ADA 10
Radio Radio/Tiny Steps	October 78	Radar ADA 24
Talking In The Dark/Wednesday Week (Free at London Dominion show)	December 78	Radar RG 1
Oliver's Army/My Funny Valentine	January 79	Radar ADA 31
Watching The Detectives (Live)/Alison (Live): Accidents Will Happen (Live) (Bonus with 'Armed Forces' LP)	February 79	Radar SAM 90
Accidents Will Happen/Talking In The Dark: Wednesday Week	May 79	Radar ADA 35
I Can't Stand Up For Falling Down/Girls Talk	March 80	F-Beat XX 1
High Fidelity/Getting Mighty Crowded	April 80	F-Beat XX 3
High Fidelity/Getting Mighty Crowded: Clowntime Is Over	April 80	F-Beat XX 3T
New Amsterdam/Dr. Luther's Assistant	June 80	F-Beat XX 5
New Amsterdam EP. New Amsterdam: Dr. Luther's Assistant/Ghost Train: Just A Memory	June 80	F-Beat XX 5E
Clubland/Clean Money: Hoover Factory	December 80	F-Beat XX 12
From A Whisper To A Scream/Luxembourg	February 81	F-Beat XX 14
Good Year For The Roses/Your Angel Steps Out Of Heaven	September 81	F-Beat XX 17
Sweet Dreams/Psycho (Live)	December 81	F-Beat XX 19
I'm Your Toy (Live)/Cry Cry Cry: Wondering	April 82	F-Beat XX 21
I'm Your Toy (Live)/My Shoes Keep Walking Back To You: Blues Keep Calling: Honky Tonk Girl	April 82	F-Beat XX 21T
You Little Fool/Big Sister: The Stamping Ground	June 82	F-Beat XX 26
Man Out Of Time/Town Crier	July 82	F-Beat XX 28

Man Out Of Time/Town Crier: Imperial Bedroom	July 82	F-Beat XX 28T
From Head To Toe/The World Of Broken Hearts	September 82	F-Beat XX 30
Party Party/Imperial Bedroom	November 82	A&M AMS 8267
Pills And Soap/Extended Version	May 83	IMP IMP 001
Everyday I Write The Book/Heathen Town	July 83	F-Beat XX 32
Everyday I Write The Book/Heathen Town: Night Time	July 83	F-Beat XX 32T
Let Them All Talk/The Flirting Kind	September 83	F-Beat XX 33
Let Them All Talk (Extended Version)/The Flirting Kind	September 83	F-Beat XX 33T
Peace In Our Time/Withered And Died	April 84	IMP TRUCE 1
I Wanna Be Loved/Turning The Town Red	June 84	F-Beat XX 35
I Wanna Be Loved/Turning The Town Red: I Wanna Be Loved (Extended Version)	June 84	F-Beat XX 35T
The Only Flame In Town/The Comedians	August 84	F-Beat XX 37
The Only Flame In Town (Version Discotheque)/The Comedians	August 84	F-Beat XX 37T
The Only Flame In Town (Version Discotheque)/Pump It Up: Baby It's You	August 84	F-Beat XX 372
Green Shirt/Beyond Belief	April 85	F-Beat ZB 40086
Green Shirt: Beyond Belief/Green Shirt (Extended Mix)	April 85	F-Beat ZT 40086

Attractions/Steve Nieve*

Single Girl/Slow Patience	July 80	F-Beat XX 7
Arms Race/Lonesome Little Town	September 80	F-Beat XX 10
Theme Music From Outline Of A Hairdo EP: Outline Of A Hairdo: Page One Of A Dead Girl's Diary/Sparrow Crap: The Tap Dancer (Bonus with 'Mad About The Wrong Boy' LP)	September 80	F-Beat COMB 1*

Albums

My Aim Is True	July 77	Stiff SEEZ 3
This Year's Model	March 78	Radar RAD 3
Armed Forces	February 79	Radar RAD 15
Get Happy!!	March 80	F-Beat XXLP 1
10 Bloody Marys and 10 How's Your Fathers	October 80	F-Beat XXC 6
Trust	January 81	F-Beat XXLP 11
Almost Blue	October 81	F-Beat XXLP 13
Imperial Bedroom	July 82	F-Beat XXLP 17
Punch The Clock	August 83	F-Beat XXLP 19
Goodbye Cruel World	June 84	F-Beat ZL 70317
The Best Of Elvis Costello – The Man	April 85	Telstar STAR 2247

Attractions/Steve Nieve*

Mad About The Wrong Boy	September 80	F-Beat XXLP 8
Keyboard Jungle	December 83	Demon FIEND 11*

Readers seeking a comprehensive listing of Elvis Costello's
international recordings are advised to consult **Elvis Costello:
The Illustrated Disco/Biography** by Geoff Parkin (Omnibus
Press, 1984).